VICTOR McLAGLEN MOTOR CORPS MEMBERS
1935-2014
(Revised 2022)

BY RUTH H. FISHER

EDITED BY JACQUELINE HECK

Victor McLaglen Motor Corps Members
1935-2014 (Revised 2022)

Library of Congress Control Number: 2022914846
All rights reserved. Printed in the United States of America

No part of this book may be used or reproduced in any manner whatsoever
without express written consent of the author, except brief quotations
embodied in critical articles or reviews.

For information:
Ruth Fisher
rthfisher4@gmail.com
www.thevmmc.com
Menifee, California, U.S.A.

Book Cover Design
By Barbara Fail, Studio 14 Productions, Madrid, NM
barbfail1@gmail.com

ISBN 978-0-9976011-2-1
Ruth H. Fisher
Victor McLaglen Motor Corps Members
1935-2014 (Revised 2022)

PREFACE

In this revision of the original book, I've added more members and more information I received from friends and relatives who read the first book. It was exciting to receive this data and pictures about these members, and it was heart-warming to see the pride with which these family members shared their input.

This Members book is an accompaniment to *The Amazing Victor McLaglen Motor Corps* (Fisher, 2016) book entered into the Library of Congress in Washington, D.C. and available at online booksellers. It specifically deals with the individual members of the Motor Corps from 1935-2014 and is a listing of all the members for whom I have information or photographs.

There are those who might have been members, but are not listed because I only knew a name and no other information. That's unfortunate, but since more than 85 years have passed since the formation of the team, it's no wonder that some of the information is a bit sketchy. After all, these guys were more interested in riding motorcycles than doing paperwork!

I've also added new appendices. These are collections of works either written by our members or about our members. I hope you enjoy this addition.

Again, if you have more information about any of these members or other members, please let me know. I'd love to know more. Happy browsing!

Thanks,
Ruth H. Fisher
Victor McLaglen Motor Corps
Former Announcer &
Honorary Life Member
rthfisher4@gmail.com

I am dedicating this book to three people
who have meant and continue to mean the world to me …
Harry, Marty and Josh Fisher

ACKNOWLEDGEMENTS

My sincere appreciation to my friend, Jacque Heck, for her many hours spent editing and proofreading. We both wanted this revised book to be the very best it could be. We spent hours giggling, laughing, cursing and crying, but the motivation never left us. I'm grateful to Jacque for her skill, advice and knowledge. I couldn't have done this final revision without her in my corner.

I'm also indebted to photographers Sam Jones, Ken Graeb and others who took the many pictures shared in this book and *The Amazing Victor McLaglen Motor Corps* (Fisher, 2016). Some of the older photos are not the best quality, and several were snapshots taken with an old instamatic or polaroid cameras (remember those?), or a cell phone camera. Plus, numerous were pried from old scrapbooks, or folded-up newspaper or magazine articles. I wish they were better, but they are what they are. The important thing is the photographs are included for your enjoyment. The text is important, but the pictures tell the real story of the expertise and professionalism forever demonstrated by the members of the Victor McLaglen Motor Corps.

I also want to recognize and thank the friends and relatives of our past and present team members who, after reading the original book, sent additional information and pictures. It was exciting to hear from every one and it made this book more inclusive.

Lastly, I cannot send this book to print until I do a proper "shout out" to my husband, Patrick Casey. Patrick was patient and helpful as Jacque and I spent hours researching and revising this book. He fixed meals, ran errands and served us a martini when the going got really tough. He continues to motivate me, and has done so much to keep the story and traditions of the VMMC alive.

TABLE OF CONTENTS

Preface i
Acknowledgement ii
Table of Contents iii
Early team 1
Members (Listed Alphabetically) 2-108
Appendix A - Mike Betschart 109
Appendix B - Bruce Chubbuck 113
Appendix C - Nick DeRush 118
Appendix D - Fred Fahnestock 122
Appendix E - Harry Fisher 124
Appendix F - Marty Fisher 132
Appendix G - Fr. Frank Hicks 133
Appendix H - Bob Holbrook 136
Appendix I - Johnny Kazian 137
Appendix J - Mickey Minor 139
Appendix K - Ray Phillips 141
Appendix L - Hap Ruggles 143
Appendix M - Tom Scott 146
Appendix N - Maria Willers 152
Appendix O - World War II & How It Affected the Victor McLaglen Motor Corps ... 162
Appendix P - Miscellaneous Articles 1930s-1940s 174
Epilogue 195

Victor McLaglen Motor Corps (VMMC)

The VMMC of the late 1930s was 25-Members Strong

More than 300 Motor Corps members performed with the Victor McLaglen Motor Corps during the 79 years from 1935 to 2014. The following pages are 311 of these members and whatever information I could collect. Unfortunately, I know there are some who have been omitted, but it was definitely unintentional. I did my very best to capture each and every member.

ABRAMS, WILLIAM J (WILLIE)

Willie joined the team on September 8, 1979 at the age of 49 years and came off the membership roll in January of 1992. He was a motorcycle mechanic by trade and rode motorcycles most of his life. Willie served in the U.S. Navy from 1947 to 1951. As a Corps member, Willie rode a 1980 1300cc Harley valued (in those days) at $6000.

Times and prices certainly have changed!

AGUIRRE, ERNEST (ERNIE)

Ernie was a member of the team from 1936-1937. His membership rank was Corporal and he was one of the top stunt men. Ernie shared his love of riding with his wife, Mary, but Mary was never a Motor Corps member. Ernie also served as a motorcycle escort for funeral processions.

Ernie's wife, Mary

"Double 1-Legged Ride" Back: Ernie Motorman: Kelly Meyers

ALBRIGHT, JIM T

Jim was initially voted on to the team on October 2, 1957. He left in 1957 and returned again on August 1, 1967.

"Horse" Top: Jim Albright Motorman: Herb Harker

ALFRING, GEORGE

George's name is engraved on the World Championship Trophy (1936).

ALLEN, FRANK W

Frank was 31 years old when he was voted in on July 22, 1957. He was dropped from membership on September 23, 1958, but apparently rejoined as records indicate he quit again on February 10, 1960. According to his application, Frank was 6'3", 165 lbs., with brown eyes and brown hair. He lived in Los Angeles, was a machinist by trade and also acted as the Corps photographer when he provided portrait pictures of the members in 1959.

ALLEN, GLENN T (GT)

GT was a member from 2003-2004. He had previously ridden with the Gold Angels Motorcycle Drill Team, a Goldwing motorcycle club in San Diego, California, and decided to give our group a try. His career with the team was brief as he decided to sell his business and move to Arizona.

ALLEN, REX (SUICIDE)
Suicide was a Motor Corps Trooper First Class in the 1930s. He was also employed as a master printer and worked as a stuntman for the movies.

ALLEN, SYDNEY (SYD)
Syd was a member in 1948. He and other Corps members were enthusiastic when they were asked to pose with Bob Hope and Doris Day at the Hollywood Santa Claus Parade.

Per the January 1949 "The Enthusiast" magazine, *"Nowhere in the world does Santa Claus arrive with such pomp and ceremony as he does in Hollywood. Among the famous folk who helped escort Santa through the streets of the movie capital were Bob Hope, Doris Day and four members of the McLaglen Motorcycle Corps including W. Bengston (left) K. Rayzor, S. Eastin and Sid Allen."* Photo – Hyman Fink of PHOTOPLAY."

1948 Hollywood Santa Claus Parade
Bob Hope on a Harley
Doris Day arm-in-arm with Syd

ALLEN / KOHLER, JOSHUA (JOSH)
Josh applied for membership in 2004 at the age of 18 along with his stepdad, GT. Josh was an excellent climber and always wore a big smile, which told everyone he was having the best time of his life. Unfortunately, for us, Josh only rode with the team for a short time.

"Totem Pole"
Top: Josh
Center: Moe Elmore
Motorman: Big Mike Betschart

"Swan"
Top: Josh
Safety: Sam
Motorman: Big Mike

ALLUM, WILLIAM (BILL)

Bill was a team member in the late 1940s and early 1950s. In this photo, Harold Bettleman drives the bike; Bill Allum performs a headstand on the arms of safetyman, Nick DeRush; while Leo Costa executes a headstand on the gas tank.

"Double Headstand"
Headstand (Rear): Bill Allum
Safety: Nick DeRush
Headstand (Front): Leo Costa
Motorman: Harold Bettleman

ANDERSON, ED (Honorary Member 1960s)

Ed worked as the parts manager at Budelier Harley-Davidson in Los Angeles in the 1960s. He would keep the shop open and attended so the Motor Corps could hold their monthly meetings at the site. In addition, Ed made occasional donations which helped keep the team up and running. Because of his contributions, Ed was granted honorary membership on February 23, 1963.

ANDERSON, GEORGE

George joined the team on April 2, 1978 when the Motor Corp was reorganizing. He quit in 1981.

George was a terrific climber and made being upside down on a ladder look easy.

"P-38 Ladder"
Ladder: George Anderson
Motorman: Harry Fisher
Right: Gene French
Left: Unknown
Dragging behind: Al Ruiz

ANDERSON, KEVIN

Kevin joined the team in 1981 while his dad was a member. He was a teenager at the time with lots of energy and strength, so most of his stunts involved climbing up on the bikes and standing on the driver's shoulders.

Kevin moved to Illinois and, when the team performed a show several years later, he stepped up and participated in some of the stunts. It was apparent he hadn't lost his touch!

Kevin also represented us at an American Motorcyclist Association (AMA) Banquet in Chicago when Victor McLaglen was inducted into their Hall of Fame.

"22 Men on One Bike"
Top No. 1 Position: Kevin Anderson

ANDERSON, MICHAEL O (MIKE)

Mike applied for membership in 2008 and was voted in as a "Rookie." Unfortunately, Mike developed some serious health issues and was unable to complete his membership requirements.

ARIANTO, HERRY

Herry rode with the team a few times in 2012 including the 2012 Love Ride in Castaic Lake, California. Herry was originally from Indonesia, where his dad commanded a motorcycle stunt team so Herry already was a skilled stuntman.

Herry

AUGUSTON, FRED

Fred was voted into membership on May 18, 1980. In 1985, he developed numerous health problems which resulted in his resignation from the team.

Created by Tedd Farrell

AYALA, ANTONIO (TONY)

Tony was voted into membership on March 3, 1959 when he was 31 years old, and he quit on June 21, 1965 when he was 37. Tony was 6'1" and 155 lbs., and he rode a new 1959 Harley. He must have been the envy of all the other members!

Tony was very proud to be a United States veteran. He was also a good husband who fathered four children: Dolores, Anthony "Babe" Ayala, Gloria "Yoyo" Harris, and Jim Ayala. Dolores, the oldest daughter, did a few motorcycle tricks with her dad but never performed with the Motor Corps. When their mother, Angie, passed away in 1993, Tony later married Delaida "Adela" in St. James Catholic Church in Perris, California. His new bride said, "He showed me how much fun it was to see places and things from a motorcycle."

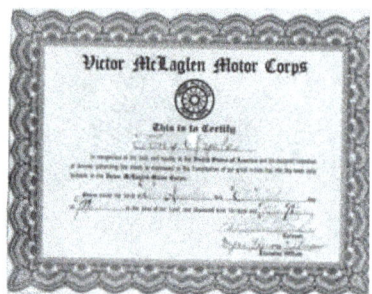

Membership Certificate March 3, 1959

(L-R) Lyle Carmody, Unknown, Dick Gerry, and Tony Ayala

Tony

(L-R) Doc Baum, Sam Watson Sr., Theron Wilmot, Cliff Hamer, Gene DeNike, Neil Irving, Lyle Carmody, Herb Harker, Tony Ayala, Cliff Taylor, Ronnie Griest, Frank Horn, Del Mar, Bill Smith

BAKER, CARL

Following retirement from the U.S. Marine Corps, Carl decided to join the Motor Corps. He was voted in on October 15, 1975 and rode a 1965 Harley.

BARRERA, DAVID
David was voted into the Motor Corps on November 22, 1987 and he rode a brand new 1987 Harley. Lucky guy!

BARRIOS, JESS JR
Jess applied for membership on August 17, 1988. His occupation was motorcycle funeral escort.

BARWICK, ED
According to membership meeting minutes, Ed was voted in on October 31, 1972. Ed was instrumental in designing and obtaining the club metal decals which screwed into the front of the helmets.

BAUM, CLAUDE A (DOC)
Doc was voted in on September 13, 1960 and was elected Vice President in 1961. Unfortunately, his term was short, as he quit on October 30, 1962.

BEHLING, HARVEY
Harvey first joined the team in 1955 but quit in 1957. He joined again in 1980 (age 66) and retired in 1996 (age 82). Harvey paid $427 for his first new Harley in 1937.

Harvey earned the distinction of being the only person to ride a motorcycle facing backward while standing on the seat; he performed this feat at the Los Angeles Coliseum. In 1980, he helped set a record riding with 22 other riders on one motorcycle at the Los Angeles Sports Arena.

Harvey

His achievements, however, were not confined to motorcycles and stunt riding. Besides being a soft-spoken guy, who worked for the Union Pacific Railroad for 32 years, he had quite an exciting life. As a pilot of a brand new single-engine Piper Cherokee, he flew around the Statue of Liberty and buzzed the Pentagon in Washington D.C. Doing that little trick today would be hazardous to your health, but Harvey managed it "back in the day."

Harvey became a motorcycle escort and had the pleasure of providing funeral procession escort services in Southern California for such celebrities as Clark Gable, Marilyn Monroe, Tyrone Power, Nat King Cole, and Al Jolson. Between 1938 and in 1983, he escorted more than 25,000 deceased to their final resting places and scattered ashes (cremains) from his airplane off the coast of Newport Beach, California (at the required 5,000 foot altitude).

Harvey

Throughout his life, Harvey managed to spice up his life with hair-raising adventures and unusual experiences riding motorcycles and flying airplanes.

BEMBARON, JOSEPH (JOE)

Joe was voted into the Motor Corp on January 9, 1973 and quit in 1975.

BENGSTON, EDWARD C (BING)

Bing joined the team around 1947. He was a photographer in the U.S. Marine Corps and, while serving with the 4th Division at Iwo Jima, he snapped some very unique photos; many of which are on display at the Smithsonian. Bing served as a VMMC Captain from 1947 to 1952. During this period of time, many of the photographs of the Motor Corps were taken by Bing.

Bing and Millie

Bing and his Motorcycle

Bing's wife, Mildred (Millie) was his strongest supporter, as was his daughter, Edonna (Eddie). Eddie provided all of the pictures and info on this page. She was also responsible for having her dad's work displayed at the Smithsonian.

Bing in Uniform

"Slow Circles"

Bing worked in aerospace at the SKUNK division at Lockheed in Burbank, CA for 30 years. According to Wikipedia, "Skunk Works is an official pseudonym for Lockheed Martin's Advanced Development Programs, formerly called Lockheed Advanced Development Projects. It is responsible for a number of aircraft designs, beginning with the P-38 Lightning in 1939 and the P-80 Shooting Star in 1943."

Bing getting ready for Showtime

BERRY, JOHN

After retiring from the United States Air Force, John bought a 1936 Harley. In 1979, the Motor Corps received a letter from Bill Dutcher who was the Director of Public Relations for the AMF Motorcycle Group. (As you may know, AMF bought out the Harley-Davidson Motor Company in 1969.) In 1981, a group of 13 investors bought back the company and the old Harley-Davidson mystique. So, back to the original story.

Bill informed us he came across someone who knew John Berry, who still owned his original 1936 Harley and was a member of the original Victor McLaglen Motor Corps team. Although we were unable to locate further information, it's a cool story; especially the fact that the gentleman had kept his Harley after all these years.

BEST, LEO

Leo's time with the Corps was short lived as he was voted in on March 17, 1964 and quit on April 17, 1964. Leo was 36 years old, worked as a plumber, lived in Long Beach, California, and rode a 1956 Harley-Davidson.

BETSCHART, ALLAN

Allan was a 15 year old high school student when he was voted in to the Corps on April 4, 1994. He quit in 1996 to move to Switzerland with his mom. Allan was the first team member to perform a stunt called the "*Walkover.*" In this stunt, his dad, Mike, would ride his motorcycle at a slow rate of speed and head straight for Allan. As Mike closed in on his intended target, Allan would step up on the front fender, then the handlebars, Mike's shoulders, down onto the rear rack and back to the ground. It happened so quickly and efficiently that it appeared Mike just drove right underneath him. Cool stunt! Because of his agility and perfect balance, Allan was often placed on the top of the Pyramid and Chariot stunts.

"High Pyramid"
Allan stands in the middle
at the half-way point

When Allan returned to the United States, he built a home in Illinois for himself and another home next door for his parents, Mike and Heidy Betschart.

BETSCHART, LOUIS MICHAEL (MIKE)

Mike was voted on to the team on November 20, 1988. Prior to retiring to Illinois, Mike owned a Mercedes Benz auto repair business in Upland, California called MB Automotive. His retirement from the Motor Corps on December 31, 2007 was a huge loss for the team. Mike was a terrific, strong motorman and he made the work of the climbers a lot easier. The list of his successful motorman-required stunts was extensive -- he could motor them all. The "*Fan*" was probably the most difficult stunt for Mike. It involved motoring nine guys, which totaled more than 1500 lbs. of weight, and he had to "muscle" them around. Incredible!

Mike passed in 2011 and he is sorely missed. (See Appendix A)

"P-38"
Motorman Mike

Mike poses on his Stunt Bike

"Human Ladder"
Motorman Mike

"Fan"
Nine Guys on One Bike
Motorman Mike

"Totem Pole"
Big Mike

BETTLEMAN, HAROLD

Harold joined the Motor Corps in 1949. As demonstrated in the photos below, Harold could do most anything on a bike.

"Shoulder Headstand"

"Double Headstand"

"Horse"

BIRDAHL, DENNIS LEE

Dennis was voted on to the team on August 23, 1966. According to his application, he was 24 years old, 6' tall and 165 lbs.

Dennis was employed as a machinist and rode a 1959 Harley 74 cubic inch.

> *This is what I heard . . . One fine summer's evening, Harry, Mike and Mark are riding back home from the bar, all three of them on Harry's motorcycle.*
>
> *Of course, they get stopped by a cop who says to them, "This motorcycle is only licensed to carry two people, and there are three of you. One of you will have to get off and walk."*
>
> *"Three of us?" says Harry as he turns to Mike. "Jeez, what happened to Marty and Mickey?"*

BLANCHETTE, GERARD ROBERT (BOB)

The membership voted Bob and his 1974 Harley on to the team on May 28, 1974. He was a machinist and made many of the slip clutches for the team bikes. Slip clutches were very important in maintaining the slow rates of speed that the members traveled while performing their stunts and riding the drill maneuvers.

Before too long, Bob started his own machine shop business and got really busy. He resigned on February 19, 1977, joined again on November 5, 1978 and quit on December 31, 1978.

BOGDA, WILLIAM

William was voted on to the team on October 15, 1956.

BRADLEY, ROBERT

This might be the person the team referred to as "young Bradley." On July 29, 1958, Mr. and Mrs. Cecil Bradley (from Pomona, California) asked if it was possible for their son to ride in some of the upcoming parades with the group. After participating in a drill practice on August 5, 1958, it was agreed that he would ride in the San Diego parade in October. According to the Corps' meeting minutes, "young Bradley" also participated in an infield show and a street parade in Anaheim.

BRECHT, JOHN CHARLES (JACK)

Jack joined the team on July 13, 2008. He indicated he had a motorcycle in his younger years, but had given it up. Prior to joining the Motor Corps, Jack worked for the Los Angeles Sheriff's Department and was a member of their posse. He retired from the Sheriff's Department after serving 20 years.

BREWER, MONTE (HONORARY MEMBER 1973)

As stated in the meeting minutes dated January, 19, 1973, "*Monte Brewer has been appointed as Honorary Member. He is allowed to participate in the stunt program only, or if on a black and white Harley, he may carry the colors in front of the team in parades, providing he has a uniform. He is also allowed to ride his present motor (Honda) in practices only.*" WHAT? A **Honda**?!

Note: Stunt List - The Stunt List is a catalog of the stunts which will be performed in the show. Each member receives a copy which is usually typed on a 5"x 7" piece of paper and taped to the gas tank for easy viewing. It is basically the same set of stunts over and over, with changes made by hand at the last minute. Changes becomes necessary when either a member doesn't appear for the show, is unable to perform a stunt (for some reason), or the leader wishes to change the line-up at the last minute.

BRILL, JACK
Jack joined the Motor Corps on January 2, 1950 and quit on February 28, 1959.

BROADBENT, JAMES V
James was voted in to membership somewhere between August 28 and October 9, 1962. He was 33 years old and he rode a 1955 Harley. His membership was short-lived as he quit on November 25, 1962. Not everyone was cut out for this kind of activity. It was best to figure that out early.

Motormen: Herb Harker & Jack Brill
Standing (L-R): Newt Fisk, Sam Watson Sr, Theron Wilmott, Chuck Schobert,
Top: Bill Smith

BROLIN, JOEL THOMAS
Joel applied for membership some time in the 1950s; there are no records showing a specific date. He worked for the Certified Grocers of California.

BROOKS, LARRY
The only records for Larry show that he joined the team on December 16, 1969.

BROSELL, RAYMOND L (DOC)
Doc was voted in to the Motor Corps on September 10, 1978 as a "medic and utility man." Doc had worked four years with the City of Los Angeles' Police Ambulance Department. A total of 23 years of emergency medical experience made him very qualified for the job! He had a 1967 Harley that pulled a little trailer with anything he needed in the event of a medical emergency.

One of Doc's favorite sayings was, "*What a revolt in development this is!*" He liked that little play on words.

BROWN, CHARLIE
Charlie was voted in to the Motor Corps on May 22, 1973 and remained a member until 1979. He performed a clown act and rode a 1972 Honda 70cc mini-bike during the shows.

BROWN, FRANK
The only records for Frank show he applied for membership on November 8, 1955 and was accepted on January 17, 1956.

BROWN, KENNETH G (KEN)
Ken was voted in to membership on May 18, 1980 and participated mostly as a motorman until about 1985 when he quit due to his wife, Linda's, bad health.

BUCKNER, CHARLES W (CHUCK)

Chuck was voted in to membership on July 22, 1979. He was a big man -- standing 6'4" and weighing a hefty 260 lbs. He worked hard to keep his 1964 Harley "steady as she goes," and he was an excellent motorman.

Chuck worked as a construction supervisor at the Southern California Water Company in Los Angeles, California, and definitely knew about hard work. In 1987, poor health caused him to resign from the team. He was definitely missed!

Chuck ready to ride

The photo above was taken in the early 1980s when the team was undergoing a reorganization. The membership roster from 1978 to 1980 increased from about five members to nearly 20 and there just weren't enough uniforms left to clothe all the men. So, they decided it was time for new, updated outfits.

During this period of transition, the members bought dark blue jumpsuits and had the "Victor McLaglen Motor Corps" printed on the back. Fullerton Harley-Davidson (currently known as Anaheim-Fullerton Harley-Davidson) purchased new helmets for the team. They ordered stick-on decals to display on the front of the helmets and the old, original red shoulder patches were sewn on the shoulders of the jumpsuits.

Most everyone had the black, police-style motorcycle riding boots and, if they didn't, they bought (or borrowed) old ones from former members. If you were a safetyman, you also had to put on a black leather belt quickly for some of the stunts (i.e., the "*Sunflower*"), where the safetyman held onto the belts of the two side men.

This became the new outfit (blue jumpsuits, white t-shirt, black riding boots, and black and white helmets). until they could afford to buy new, traditional uniforms

BUIE, LEE A JR

Lee was voted in to membership on March 7, 1961 and quit on July 18, 1961. He rode a 1950 Harley and worked as a computer operator, which (at that time) was a new occupation.

Tylor and Mickey sporting the temporary 1978 uniform

BURGIN, JAMES EDWARD

James was voted in to membership on April 10, 2010 shortly after his mother, Janis, joined the team. He was 16 years old, and he and his mom enjoyed performing stunts together. One of the long-time members, Mickey Minor, held the top spot on the "High Pyramid" for twenty years until his retirement in 2010. At that time, James replaced him and held this important position until he left the Motor Corps due to his schooling, ROTC and other commitments.

"High Pyramid"
James on top
Janis (mom) far left

"P-38"
James hanging out on the right

James Burgin

BURGIN, JANIS SUE

Janis was voted in as a member of the team on October 12, 2008. She was the third female to obtain membership with the Motor Corps and was a real asset to the team. Being slender and light weight, Janis was able to climb on shoulders and make many difficult maneuvers. In addition to her many stunts, she rode her 2005 Standard Soft Tail Harley in the Flags. Janis always had the most enthusiasm and the biggest smile and was a joy to have around.

"Chariot"
Janis on Top

Janis riding Butch's
"Mini-Me" Flag Bike

"Push-up"
Janis on Top again

BUTTERFIELD, PAUL N

Paul was approved for membership on May 11, 1954 and was elected Motor Corps Vice President in 1956.

CALCO, FRED

Fred was voted in to membership in 1962 at the age of 35. He rode a 1957 Harley and worked in an auto body shop.

CALDERA, CHARLES ARTHUR JR (CHUCK)

Chuck was voted in to the group as a member on May 9th and quit on September 1, 1964. He rode a 1949 Harley and was a postal worker for the United States Postal Service (USPS).

CAMARENA, FERNANDO R

Fernando first joined the team on November 4, 1990. The rules stated each member had to have his/her own motorcycle. Fernando did not, so it was necessary he drop off the team (which he did in 1991). This was too bad as Fernando was really good at climbing and going upside down.

In 2013, Fernando (once again) applied for membership and was voted in on April 27th. This time. Fernando had a bike and also brought a new and valuable member to the club – his son, Luis.

Fernando Camarena

CAMARENA, LUIS FERNANDO

Luis was voted in to membership on June 29, 2013 at the age 19. The team was looking for a top man for the Pyramid and Luis was elected! He was young, agile and able to climb to the top of the High Pyramid better than anyone. He caught on fast and was quickly accepted by his teammates.

Luis Camarena

CARMODY, LARRY LEE

Larry was officially voted in to membership on November 11, 1980 and quit on October 30, 1981. Larry was the son of long-time member, Lyle Carmody.

> *Note: There are three (3) basic positions on most multiple-person stunts: (1) The Motorman who has control of the motorcycle, (2) The Safetyman who assists and protects the climber, and (3) The Climber, who stands on shoulders, goes upside down or hangs off the sides.*

CARMODY, LYLE I (LYLE)

Lyle Carmody

Lyle was voted on to the team by the membership on June 1, 1951 and he quit on July 13, 1965. Professionally, Lyle was the first motorcycle traffic reporter for radio station KMPC in Los Angeles, California. Not only was he a celebrity, but he did an exceptional job performing as an excellent motorman and keeping the administrative tasks of the Motor Corps team under control. He was elected Secretary in 1956, 1957, 1958 and served as the Secretary/Treasurer in 1961. In 1978, when the team was going through a reorganization, Harry asked Lyle if he would return, take care of the paperwork and help enforce the rules. He agreed and stayed active with the team until 1981 when he officially retired. At the next Annual Awards Banquet, he was presented with a Lifetime Membership card.

Lyle on his Harley with the KMPC Radio team

"2-Man Pushup"
Motormen: Lyle Carmody, Smitty Smith, Joe Militello

CASPER, MIKE

Mike joined the team in 1965.

"P-38 Human Ladder"
Created by Tedd Farrell

Mike Casper (right) receives Motor Corps Membership Certificate from Colonel Herb Harker

CASTRO, LARRY
Larry joined the team on August 23, 1981 and became inactive in 1987.

CATES, GETCHEL (SKEETS)
Skeets' name is engraved on the 1936 World Championship Trophy along with rest of the stunt team.

CATFORD, MIKE
Mike joined the team on August 10, 1965 and quit around 1971. He served as President in 1968 and 1969, and Vice President in 1970.

CHAVEZ, BENJAMIN GARCIA (BEN)
Ben was voted in to membership on August 11, 1985 and became inactive in 1987.

"Half P-38"
Left: Mike Catford
Motorman: Butch Ferrell

Created by Tedd Farrell

CHUBBUCK, MALCOLM BRUCE (BRUCE)

Bruce was voted in to the Motor Corps on April 2, 1978. He first heard about the team in 1947 when his dad, S. E. "Chubby" Chubbuck, co-owner of the Harley-Davidson dealership in Pasadena, told him about a hill climb race where the Victor McLaglen Motor Corps (VMMC) would be performing (north of Saugus on State Highway 6, which is now Highway 14). It featured four motorcycles, side-by-side, racing up the hill. He and his father were told to find racer, Nick DeRush, when they got there. Nick was the leader of the VMMC. They found Nick just in time to see Nick's friend and coworker, Bob Ayriss, win the first race.

Bruce began riding a 1948 Harley-Davidson 125cc in December 1947 at age 17. By 1978, after years of riding on the street, he was leading the color guard unit of the now reorganized VMMC and carrying the American flag at all of our shows.

Beginning with the reorganization of the team under the new leadership of Harry Fisher, Bruce was one of the key backbone members of the team. He helped to rejuvenate the team and get the "ball rolling" … so to speak. He took over the Treasurer position, headed up the flag unit and became a liaison between the Harley-Davidson Motor Company and the Motor Corps. While on the team, Bruce rode various bikes including a 1974 HD X90 Mini Bike, Harry Fisher's 1933 Harley VL, his own 1936 Harley 61 OHV, and his 1991 Harley FLHTC dresser.

Bruce poses with his 1991 FLHTC

Bruce proudly displays the American flag while riding his Mint 1936 Knucklehead

CHUBBUCK, MALCOLM BRUCE (BRUCE) (Cont'd)

In the 1990s, Bruce and Marty Fisher performed the "Half P-38" stunt with Bruce hanging off the side and Marty Fisher driving. At that time, Bruce was the oldest member (in his early 60s) and Marty was the youngest (in his early 20s). Very trusting for a gent Bruce's age to put all his trust in a young 20 year old! (See Appendix B.)

"Half P-38"
Left: Bruce Chubbuck
Motorman: Marty Fisher

Bruce in the '80s with his 1936 Harley EL Flag Bike

Bruce 20+ years later – same bike!

CLAYTON, CHARLES REY (CHUCK)
Chuck was voted in to membership on November 5, 1975. He rode a 1967 Harley.

COHEN, JAY
Jay was accepted for membership on April 7, 1986. The next step was to immediately paint his 1982 red Harley in the uniform black and white colors.

Jay left the team in January of 1992.

COOK, BUD
Bud's name is engraved on the 1936 World Championship Trophy.

COSTA, LEO
Leo was a member of the team from the 1940s through the 1960s. In addition to being a motorman, he performed a stunt which involved him performing a handstand on the handlebars.

COWEN, TOM
Tom was voted in by the membership on April 2, 1978 as part of the new reorganization.

Motorman: Leo Costa
Top: Ray Green

Created by Tedd Farrell

CRAWFORD, JAMES (JIMMY)

Joining the team in 1935 makes Jimmy one of the original members of the team. The photos below show Jimmy performing headstands. In an interview with a local newspaper, Jimmy – with a note of enthusiasm in his voice – said, *"Show business is a lot of fun. It has something that you can't get anywhere else, the thrill of doing something well before a group of people. What kind of show business am I in? I'm a motorcycle stunt rider. I've been with the Victor McLaglen Motor Corps since its inception in October 1935."*

"Headlight Headstand"
Upside Down: Jimmy Crawford
Motorman: Wayne Fitzgerald
Right: Hap Ruggles
Left: Joe Stewart

"Stretcher Handstand"

Jimmy continued by saying, *"None of the fellows on the team do it for the business end of it, but rather for the thrill of showing off before an interested audience. The majority of them have been racers or stuntmen before and can't get the feel of the show out of their system, so they do this for a hobby. We have had very few accidents since the team's inception. We have a few spills, but they're all in fun."*

According to other articles, Crawford was an affable, seemingly nerveless person. He was of medium height and weight, and his ruddy complexion was accented by slightly red hair. He came to California from Minnesota and graduated from Manual Arts High School. He worked in a carnival for two seasons, rode a motorcycle in the motordrome, traveled as an oiler on a ship for a year, and worked as a tool and die maker at Douglas Aircraft Company. Jimmy's name is engraved on the World Championship Trophy.

CRAWFORD, JOHN G

John joined the team on January 24, 1956. Little else is known except that John lived in South Gate and he signed the Civil Defense volunteer statement. Whether Jimmy and John Crawford were brothers is also unknown.

CRAWFORD, RALPH L

Ralph applied for membership; however, the actual date and whether he was actually voted on to the team is unknown. The date had to have been during the time Herb Harker was a member as Herb signed as his sponsor.

Ralph worked for Ralph M. Parsons Company in downtown Los Angeles and also signed the Civil Defense volunteer statement.

CUPPETT, LESLIE (LES)

Les was voted in to membership on November 27, 1962. He was 38 years old at the time and he rode a 1956 Harley.

In 1964, he was elected Vice President and Executive Board member of the Corps, but he quit in 1965.

1964 Awards Banquet
L-R: Cliff Hamer, Les Cuppett,
Colonel Kuri, Harry Fisher, Lyle Carmody

DAVIES, ROGER SCOTT

Roger was voted in on July 23, 1978 and quit in 1985. He rode a 1972 Harley FLH and he was a motorman. Professionally, Roger worked as a truck driver for City Freight Lines in Los Angeles, California.

Roger Davies

Riding "Drill"

Roger in Uniform
Ready to Ride

"Rear Rack Ride"

DAVIS, HARRY ROY

Harry applied for membership some time in the 1950s. Records indicate he attended a meeting on January 17, 1956 and requested, and was given, an "Inactive" card at a meeting on July 31, 1956.

DAVIS, RUSSELL E (RUSS)

Russ was voted in to membership as the Team Announcer on March 31, 1990. Russ rode a 1980 Harley FLH and worked as the parts manager at Fontana Motorcycle, Inc

DAY, CLARENCE (SONNY)

Sonny joined the team in the mid-1970s and quit in 1981. He was a good motorman and safetyman, and could always be counted on to have a lot of fun.

DELEO, RONALD (RON)

Ron was voted in to membership on October 15, 1975, at the age of 35, and resigned from the Corps on February 18, 1977. He rode a 1968 Harley and lived in Long Beach.

DENIKE, GENE

July 12, 1960 was the date Gene was granted membership.

DERUSH, DON LEE

Don was Nick DeRush's oldest son. He rode with the team for a bit but was killed in a motorcycle accident in 1959 when he was 26 years old.

Don Lee DeRush

Created by Tedd Farrell

DeRUSH, TRUMAN WARD (NICK)

Captain Truman (Nick) Ward DeRush was instrumental in the establishment of the Victor McLaglen Motor Corps in 1935. As a motorcycle stuntman, Nick had the opportunity to communicate with numerous actors. It was during one of these occasions that he was able to convince the Academy Award winning film star, Victor McLaglen, to sponsor the first team and, thus, the Victor McLaglen Motor Corps (VMMC) was born.

Nick was the leader of the group from 1935 to 1952, and his affiliation with Hollywood and the movies enabled him to meet Victor McLaglen and to use his business manager for booking venues to demonstrate the team's skills. He led the team in drill maneuvers, performed and acted as a motorman on numerous stunts with the Corps members, and helped to build a legend.

In the photo above, Captain DeRush is posing on his 1935VL. The handlebars have been altered from the original. One of our members, Bruce Chubbuck, explained "that's easy to do with a bending tool." (Notice the bandage or cast on his left hand? Hmm! At least it's not on his "throttle" hand!)

Nick steered the team to win the World Championship trophy in a contest with Mexico City in 1936. His name is engraved on the front of the trophy along with the Corps members who performed at the competition. In those early years, he also headed up the team on a west coast tour by train, where they performed shows in California, Idaho, Utah, and Oregon. Finally, he managed the VMMC in the Rose Parade, the Hollywood Santa Claus Lane Parade, and hundreds of other local exhibitions including infield shows; a movie, *Meet John Doe*; and a demonstration video for General Motors.

Captain Nick DeRush

Nick's wife Eunice

DeRUSH, TRUMAN WARD (NICK) (Cont'd)

In 1937, Chevrolet Motor Division of General Motors developed the modern-day differential and used the Motor Corps "Pinwheel" drill to demonstrate how the inside rider (as the axle of the wheel) had to go slower than the outside rider (as the outside rim of the wheel) because they have a greater distance to travel.

Video by Jam Handy Organization

Screen-shot of team demonstrating differential concept

Some stunts shown at beginning of YouTube video

To see the whole video, search for General Motors Differential on YouTube. It's only 9:31 minutes long and very interesting.

We've heard lots of stories about Nick. One we know is true is when he was employed at Rich Budelier's Los Angeles Harley-Davidson, which (at that time) was the largest motorcycle dealer on the Pacific Coast. He was the manager, one of the leading salesmen and the head of their Rider Activity Club.

Nick was born on October 3, 1908 in Colorado and his given name was Truman Ward DeRush. Nick and his wife, Eunice, had four sons, Truman, Don, Gilbert and Damon. Nick passed away in Trona, California on January 6, 1962 and is interred at Inglewood Park Cemetery in Inglewood, California. (See Appendix C)

Nick's Business Card

DESCOTEAUX, ARTHUR J (ART)
Art was voted in on January 9, 1954 and resigned on April 19, 1957 due to health issues.

Art worked at North American Aviation in El Segundo, California.

DIZACOMO, JOSEPH (JOE)
Joe became a member on October 10, 1961 at the age of 34, and he quit on July 9, 1963. He was originally from Boston Massachusetts, and worked as a truck driver.

Joe was pretty unique. He was always upbeat, always had a big smile on his face and was always ready to play tricks on you. Most people didn't know Joe was missing one leg which was fitted with a prosthetic. There were occasions when a new guy would go to lift Joe on a "Push-up" and walk away saying, *Hey, did you know that guy has a wooden leg?* Joe wouldn't let him know ahead of time, and got a big chuckle afterward!

His handicap never slowed him down. He was able to do most any stunt and ride his 1950 Harley in the drills just as good as the next guy.

DOAKS, FREDRICK W (FRED)
Fred was voted in as a member of the Corp on December 16, 1969.

DOTZENROD, WILLIAM ERIC (BILL)
In 1986, 16-year-old Bill joined the Motor Corps as a mini-bike rider. He'd been hanging around for several years with his mom, who married long-time member, Dick Gerry. Bill always had a big smile on his face and was ready to do whatever the members asked.

His primary job was to make sure the crowds did not step out in front of any of the oncoming stunts. He was definitely an asset to the team as he rode his mini-bike for safety along, beside and just ahead of the big stunts in the parades.

DOUGLAS, KENNETH (CURLEY)
Curley was voted into membership in 1955.

DOYLE, STEVEN (STEVE)
Steve was voted into the Motor Corps on November 22, 1987 and resigned on July 21, 1990.

He rode a 1978 Harley.

DOYLE, THOMAS (TOM)
Tom applied for membership on September 7, 1988 when he was 17 years old. No further information is available regarding his membership status or activity.

DRAHOS, HARVEY

Harvey was a member in the 1940s. In 2002, Harvey wrote, *"I graduated from Garfield High School (California) in 1941. The team practiced at the Polo Grounds on Riverside Drive. I am now 80, so have slowed down a bit."*

Harvey enjoyed riding his 1939 80HF (picture below shows him and his mom on back). This was his transportation to and from the Infantry Training Center in Camp Roberts, California.

1939 80FH
Harvey and Mom

1946 Harley
Harvey Drahos

WWII and Corps Members gather for a Mini-Reunion
Jim Dylerly, Harvey Drahos and Harvey Behling

DUMONT, ANDREW H (ANDY)

Andy was voted in to membership on March 23, 1980. He was with the team for just one year, when he quit to take a job as director of a "comprehensive substance abuse program" at the Coeur d'Alene Indian Reservation in northwestern Idaho.

DUNHAM, WAYNE

Wayne was a member in 1941. One of his performances with the Team included a charity event honoring the late Howard Jones, who was a University of Southern California football coach who died at age 55. Howard Jones was a member of the College Football Hall of Fame's inaugural class of inductees in 1951.

The show paid tribute to his memory and the Motor Corps performed in front of an audience of 50,000 fans at the Los Angeles Coliseum. This event was the first to be held in the Coliseum since Jones' death, and it included three hours of star-studded entertainment. Red Skelton was Master of Ceremonies and Gloria Jean sang the Star-Spangled Banner. Other famous celebrities in attendance were Mickey Rooney, Susanna Foster, Andy Devine, Charles (Buddy) Rogers, Ann Miller, Borrah Minnevitch and the Harmonica Rascals.

According to a newspaper account of the event, *"Only mishap of the evening occurred during stunting by two members of the Victor McLaglen Motor Corps. Standing on his hands, Wayne Dunham slipped from the shoulders of Hap Ruggles, who was driving, and was carried from the field with a fractured arm."*

ELLIS, LESLY (LES)

Les was voted in on February 12, 1993.

At the time, he worked as an auto mechanic maintaining the limousines and other vehicles for Harry Fisher's transportation business. He was initially introduced to the Motor Corps through Harry and, voila, he became a member. Funny how that happens!

Les had a severe case of rheumatoid arthritis; however, he ignored it, took his meds and look what he could do!

Les Ellis

Motorman: Harry Fisher
Left: Les Ellis
Right: Dick Gerry

"Shoulder Layback"
Motorman: Bob Jensen
Top: Les Ellis

ELLIS, LES (Cont'd)

In 1996, the team went to Reno, Nevada to perform with the Motor Corps. Les, however, had something else on his mind. He planned to marry Joyce and wanted the rest of the team to be in attendance.

So, we all piled into our rental cars and drove over to a little chapel someone had found. After a brief wait outside, while another couple "tied the knot," we all went inside for the festivities.

Our eldest member, Dick Gerry, walked Joyce down the aisle; someone found a flower for her to carry; the members' wives were the bridesmaids; and our little poodle and mascot, Patches, was the flower girl. What a sight we all were. But, it worked. They were "hitched" and we all went to a restaurant for a real celebration!

Later, Les worked as an escort for funeral processions in the Los Angeles area until he retired and moved to Silver City, New Mexico.

Motorman Escort: Dick Gerry
Left: Lovely Bride Joyce
Not Pictured: Waiting Groom Les

Created by Tedd Farrell

ELMORE, JACOB (JAKE)

Jake was 16 years old when he was voted in on July 21, 2002. His dad, Moe, was a member of the team, so the two of them made a great father-son duo! In the beginning, Jake rode the team's Harley-Davidson Whizzer motorized bicycle. It wasn't too long before he got his own Harley, and was able to participate in the drills and stunts.

"Front Fender Layback" Motormen Jake & Dad Moe Elmore

Jake's early days on the H-D Whizzer

Jake gets his new bike …

then a regulation paint job & uniform!

ELMORE, MICHAEL KEITH (MOE)

The Corps voted Moe on to the team on October 31, 1999. Moe did a great job as a safetyman and in drills. He rode a hand-shift 1951 EL model Harley and was the envy of all.

Moe Elmore

"Bridge"
Motorman: Mike Betschart
Front Safety: Sam Watson
Seat Safety: Frank Hicks
Rear Rack Safety: Moe Elmore
Upside Down: Mickey Minor

Marty Fisher & Moe Riding in Pairs

ERICKSON, BAKER E

Baker was accepted into the Corps on May 14, 1957. Professionally, he worked for the Union Pacific Railroad.

ERICKSON, PHIL

Phil was a member of the Corps from 1948 through 1952. A recent note from Ed Phillips, a VMMC member, described a three-man-high stunt which was performed on a dirt track. During the stunt, Phil cracked his spine. Nevertheless, he completed the performance and drove off with the rest of the team. What a man!

EVANS, CLIVE E (TED)
Ted was voted in to membership on November 22, 1987 and rode in the Flag Unit.

EVORS, WILLIAM E (EARL)
Earl served as the Motor Corps Secretary from January through September 1956. He worked for Constructors Transportation.

FAHNESTOCK, FRED H and HAROLD
Fred joined the team on April 27, 1939 when he was just 15 years old. It is interesting to note that his membership certificate was personally signed by Victor McLaglen. Fred and his brother, Harold, are shown performing a two-motor pyramid (photo on right). In the November 1938 issue of *The Enthusiast*, Hap Ruggles wrote, "The Fahnestock boys just returned from Chicago riding two new motorcycles."

"High Pyramid"

In 2018, his son, Jim, wrote to say Fred had passed away; he was 105 years old. (See Appendix D)

I asked Bruce Chubbuck if he could identify Fred's stunt bike (see photo on right). Bruce said, *"I have studied this picture and my guess is it is a 1939 Harley 74UL flathead. It had the changes that the 1936 61OHV had. It had the double tube frame, return oil pump and hard steel welded gas tanks. In 1936, the VL (74 Flat) had a 4-Speed Transmission but, in 1937, the UL had the same 4-speed that was in the 61OHV because of the double tube frame. It looks like it has the new tail light. For some dumb reason, they put neutral between second and third gear and that looks like where the shift lever is if it was in neutral. If it was a 61 OHV, the air cleaner would be on the other side. The 1940s had an aluminum brake handle."* Thanks, Bruce.

15 year old Fred

Fred Fahnestock

FARRELL, DELAIN E (BUTCH)
Butch was voted in to the Corps on December 10, 1969. He was a member of the Executive Board (E-Board) and Secretary in 1970.

> *NOTE: The Motor Corps E-Board consisted of up to nine (9) members: Colonel, Drill Leader, Secretary, Treasurer, top three (3) ranking members, and two (2) elected members who represented the membership. They listened to complaints, suggestions and grievances; acted on them accordingly; and reported back to the membership.*

FARRELL, TEDDY G (TEDD)

Up to now, you've no doubt seen Tedd Farrell's name mentioned on more than one occasion. That is because Tedd was a very talented guy. Tedd created a new cartoon about the Corps and presented it to his teammates every Christmas. We always looked forward to what he'd come up with next! We're lucky to have saved many of his drawings/cartoons and are able to share them with you throughout this book.

Tedd Farrell

Tedd was voted in to the Motor Corps on June 7, 1985. He was a retired Deputy Sheriff and had ridden with the Escondido Police Motorcycle Drill Team. Tedd said "… *he had a strong desire to be a part of an 'elite,' well-trained group of fellow Motorcyclists.*" He also claimed to be a "Certified Harley Fanatic Collector" and stated he had collected over 40 bikes.

Tedd remembered a time when the Motor Corps performed for the Sturgis 50th Anniversary. John Moser, a member of the Seattle Cossacks team, never let anyone else ride his vintage Harley, so Harry played a joke on him. During the Seattle Cossacks show (they are a premier motorcycle stunt and drill team, too), VMMC member Ruben Pantoja and another accomplice put on dresses and went out in the middle of the field to distract John. While he was distracted, Harry jumped on John's bike and rode it around and around the show area until John finally gave up and started laughing!

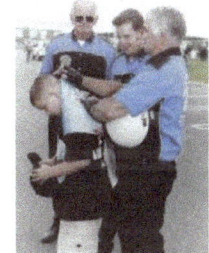

(L-R) Jake Elmore, Bruce Chubbuck & Tedd Farrell

Autograph signing for a young fan!
Sam Watson - Left
Marty Fisher – Middle
Tedd Farrell - Signing

FARRELL, WARREN

Warren was a member from 1985-1987. He was a teenager at that time and son of member, Ted Farrell. Warren rode a mini-bike in the team. Mini-bikes were used for safety and crowd control during the performances.

FENTON, JAMES (JIMMY)

Jimmy joined the team in the early 1940s and continued at least until 1949.

FERRY, DENNIS E

Dennis was voted in on September 13, 1974.

FISHER, HARRY M

Please indulge me with Harry's story. I know it's lengthy, but he was a formidable man, leader, husband, father, and son. There is a lot to say because he lived a lot and he did a lot. (See Appendix E)

Harry possessed a genuine love for motorcycles. In fact, it is fair to say that motorcycles were his life. At age 15, Harry had dreams of racing motorcycles at the Ascot Raceway. His mother, however, had an alternate plan to prevent him from the dangers of racing. In order to create a distraction, she contacted Herb Harper, the current leader of the Victor McLaglen Motor Corps, and convinced him to allow Harry to join the team. The rest is history and the saga continues …

Harry was first voted into membership on December 4, 1962 when he was 17 years old. In 1965, he acted as Secretary before assuming his role as Stunt Leader. Eventually, in 1978, he became Colonel and leader of the Victor McLaglen Motor Corps – a position he admirably maintained until his death in 2014.

Harry was a busy guy and he didn't waste time. At age 21, he had accumulated a portfolio of organizational memberships which included the Victor McLaglen Motor Corps, the Huntington Park Elks Lodge, the Hollywood Masonic Lodge, the Southern California Motorcycle Club, the Sidehack Association and the American Motorcycling Association … and he actively participated in all of them.

The photo (below right) shows Harry at the Big Bear Parade sporting his VMMC uniform and riding Cliff Hamer's 1933 VL Harley, which he eventually purchased from Cliff.

Lyle Carmody and Harry Fisher
1964 VMMC Annual Banquet

Harry Fisher
1963 Parade
Big Bear, California

FISHER, HARRY M (Cont'd)

In 1966, Harry performed his first Firewall Crash with the Victor McLaglen Motor Corps team. He, subsequently, did a number of successful Firewall Crashes with the Huntington Park Elk and the VMMC teams.

"Firewall Crash"
Rider: Harry Fisher

Ground-Level Thunder Event
Casa de Fruta, California 1996

It was October 1996 when Harry Fisher (driving) and *Thunder Press* editor, Reg Kittrelle (riding on back), performed a successful and spectacular "Firewall Crash" as shown in the picture (right).

On June 27, 1967, Harry quit the VMMC. Actually, he was "booted out" because they discovered him practicing one evening with the Huntington Park Elks Motorcycle Stunt and Drill Team. He and his buddy of wing-walking fame, Johnny Kazian, both decided they would quit the Victor McLaglen team and join the Elks team. Within a couple of years with the Elks team, Harry was promoted to drill leader, which was the second position under the Colonel. Because of the Colonel's affiliation as a Past Exalted Ruler at the Elks Lodge, many of the Elks motorcycle team events were supported by the Lodge. This was important because the team was financially supported by the Lodge and they were also able to obtain a fee from the promoters to support the finances associated with travel, insurance and equipment costs to perform shows.

At that time, the VMMC team was against charging for their services. Also, wherever the Elks performed, there was usually an Elks Lodge nearby and we would go there after the show to "unwind." The down side, however, was that the California Elks Charter wouldn't allow the team to perform outside California. We did 20-30 shows each year all within the state. At the end of the year, any excess funds from our performances were donated to the Elks' charity, Cerebral Palsy.

FISHER, HARRY M (Cont'd)

The 1970s were a particularly busy time for Harry. And, yet, he still managed to make it to practice each week and perform in all the shows. He attended truck driving school to receive his Commercial Driver's License, quit a delivery job he had at Rapid Blue Print Company to work at Hadley Auto Transport delivering new Ford cars throughout the west coast, transitioned discretely between the Huntington Park Elks Motorcycle Stunt and Drill Team and the Victor McLaglen Motor Corps, moved to Sylmar and started a motorcycle repair business (with a partner), worked as a motorcycle funeral escort during the day (when possible), cared for his bride, fathered a new son, and did everything he could to support his family (personally and financially) … and the list goes on.

Since the VCMM was doing about 30-plus parades and several infield shows each year that needed him to be there and because getting time off work was difficult, he resorted to taking lots of "sick" days from work and visiting an "ailing aunt" so he could attend the practices and shows while also taking care of business (all of it)!

The photos below show Harry (early 1970s) perfecting his stunts on his 1963 Harley Panhead while leading the Huntington Park Elks Motorcycle Stunt and Drill Team.

"Pivot Slow Circle"
Motorman: Harry Fisher
Top: Walt Houser
Bottom: Clown, Tony Barbaro

"Slow Circle"
Motorman: Harry Fisher
Front Axle: Joe Smith
Handstand : Walt Hauser

Note: "Slow Circles" are when the rider maneuvers the motorcycle into a very tight slow circles, sometimes taking his hands off the handlebars but NEVER putting his foot down on the pavement. A new rider will practice hours and hours before perfecting this stunt.

FISHER, HARRY M (Cont'd)

More photos of Harry performing with the Elks Motorcycle Stunt and Drill Team.

"Backward Ride"   *"Frame Ride"*

It was 1978 when Harry received a call from Herb Harker, Colonel of the Victor McLaglen Motor Corp. Herb asked Harry to drop by because he wanted to talk to him. Well, since Herb and Harry hadn't spoken to one another for about ten years, this certainly caught Harry's attention. So, Harry and I met with Herb at his house for a little coffee and a chat. Herb said he wanted to retire from the Motor Corps and move to Illinois, and he wanted Harry to take over his management position for the team.

Well, Harry said he'd give it some thought. We went home and, after about two seconds of "thought" and an additional day (so he wouldn't appear too anxious), he called Herb and told him he would be happy to manage the team.

This same year, Harry got out of the motorcycle repair business, opened his own motorcycle funeral escort business, bought and ran J. C. Armature business and moved the family to Cerritos, California so he could lead the VMMC.

Some time in the 1980s, Harry received a call from someone in the advertising business. They were looking for motorcycle riders who could do drill maneuvers for a television advertisement. They had heard of Harry and wondered if he would be interested. After a bit of negotiations, Harry rounded up a few of his friends (who, by the way, were also members of the VMCC) and they all headed to Provo, Utah to do a Budweiser commercial. They were going to make "big bucks." Hmmm, cold beer and big bucks … what a delightful combination!

FISHER, HARRY M (Cont'd)

Kirby Frymoyer, Ray Kult, Nick Oliver, Don Warren and Harry loaded themselves into our van and headed to Utah. The storyline of the commercial was that the Shriner look-alikes (which were Harry and his team of cyclists) were in Brigham (a fake town) performing in a parade. Suddenly, a bad biker gang rode into town and started harassing them. After a few minutes, they all got together, drank a Bud and the commercial ended.

The comical thing was that one of the actors, who was portraying a bad biker, was actually snubbing Harry and his group of look-alikes. So, it appeared the "harassing" part of the commercial required little or no acting on the part of the "bad biker." The bad biker was making rude comments about their pointy-toed shoes and funny hats.

Suddenly, the rude/bad biker couldn't get his "kick-start" Harley going and everyone was standing around waiting for him. Harry, nonchalantly, walked over and asked if he needed some help.

Left: Bad Biker BUDdy (Actor)
Right: Harry Fisher

The guy said, *"What makes you think you can start this thing if I can't?"* Harry said, *"Try me."* So, Harry swung his leg with the pointy-toed shoes over the bike, gave it a few good kicks and -- lo and behold -- it started right up! After that, they became best Buds – no pun intended. Cool story!

Fake town of Brigham

Harry Fisher, Kirby Frymoyer,
Ray Kult, Nick Oliver, and Don Warren

They made some extra bucks, got to star in a TV commercial and had a heck of a good time! They never made the BIG bucks, though!

FISHER, HARRY M (Cont'd)

Harry and his miniature poodle, Patches, were inseparable and were often seen riding the bike together. Patches went everywhere with Harry, and she was a real asset in gaining attention and popularity at the shows; especially with the children. A couple of days after we had rescued Patches, we discovered she was deaf. She quickly learned sign language and adapted to motorcycle riding. At one of the shows (I believe it was New York City), a spectator approached me and said, "*I know you love your dog and she looks really cute in the show, but I'm concerned about her hearing. With your husband blowing that whistle right by her ears, it probably hurts her and she may go deaf.*" Apparently, he hadn't been listening to me when I mentioned on the microphone that Patches was a little, **deaf**, rescue dog. I'm still not sure he believed me.

Show time for Patches and Harry

Maria, Harry and Patches practicing riding in 2's (or maybe 3's?)

Harry rode his 1963 Harley Panhead (with a hand-shift) for many years; that was, of course, until his son, Marty, started riding and took it over. Then, Harry began riding his 1951 rigid frame with a hand-shift and suicide clutch. He drove all the stunts on this bike including the "Roman Ride" stunt, where he rode two bikes at the same time.

Harry's 1951 Panhead Rigid Frame Harley

FISHER, HARRY M (Cont'd)

The "Roman Ride"
Harry Fisher riding his 1951 and his son's 1964

Harry and his 1951 Harley Stunt Bike
2012 Performance
Simi Valley, California

Harry at practice …
La Palma, CA - 2011
… always with the whistle in his mouth!

Harry passed away on March 13, 2014 at 68 years old. He had driven a semi-truckload of brand new Harley-Davidson motorcycles to Florida for the Daytona Bike Week festivities. He was doing what he loved, had met up with longtime friends at the event and was having a good time.

Unfortunately, his heart just couldn't take all that fun and enjoyment, and it gave out on him. It was a shock to many across the country, and his quick laugh, fun and persuasive ways will always be missed. He was a genuine leader, an excellent motorcyclist, a wonderful husband, and a super father and grandfather.

Rest in peace, Harry.

FISHER, MARTIN M (MARTY)

Actually, Marty began hanging with the team at about age five. However, on May 21, 1989 (when he was only 15 years old), he was officially voted into membership. At that time, he was the youngest member to be accepted into the Corps.

Marty is the son of the leader, Harry, and his wife, Ruth (the author of this book). Marty was an extremely talented motorcycle rider and motored for many other stunts which required superb control of the motorcycle. In fact, by the age of 17, he was one of the four principal High Pyramid motormen.

Marty Fisher 2010

"High Pyramid" Motorman Marty

"2005 Honda's Ride for Kids" Torrance, CA (L-R) Marty Fisher, Jake Elmore, Tylor Hick & and Sue Hutchings

In the beginning, Marty rode a mini-bike before graduating to his dad's 1964 Harley. He rode that Harley with the team through most of his high school and college years, and while he was also employed at Anaheim-Fullerton Harley-Davidson. Few of his college buddies at San Diego State University ever knew he performed with a famous motorcycle stunt team. When Friday arrived, he'd just say, "Gotta go home and visit the parents this weekend." He'd drive home, get ready to go out of town for a performance, return home on Sunday evening, and make the return drive of 121 miles back to San Diego State in time for his classes on Monday morning! His buddies never knew.

Marty at show in San Francisco at the Presidio

Marty at show in Ohio

Marty Fisher RAMS Locker Room St. Louis, Missouri

FISHER, MARTIN M (MARTY) (Cont'd)

In 1996, when the team was performing in Denver (one of the trips that Marty sneaked away from his college life for), we did our 10:00 am show, then jumped in a couple of our rental cars and drove the 15 or so miles to Golden, Colorado to take a quick tour of the Coors Brewing Company.

It was a very interesting tour and we did manage to taste the product before we left. We got back to the convention center just in time for the 2:00 pm show. (I don't think Harry was real impressed with this little escapade, but we were in the area, so why not!)

"Yep, I can do stunts anywhere ... on any thing! Even in Colorado on a burro"

"Spread Eagle" Practice
Tylor Hicks (Middle)
Mike Betschart & Marty Fisher

"Frame Ride"
Marty on his 1964 Harley

FISHER, MARTIN M (MARTY) (Cont'd)

Marty obtained his Bachelor of Science degree in Business Management at California State University, Long Beach (CSULB) in 1998. In 2001, he landed a job in the Motorcycle Division at the American Honda Motor Company in Torrance, California. He entered the company as a Western Regional Representative for the Honda Rider's Club Association (HRCA). One of his first assignments was to write an article about himself for their company magazine (see Appendix F to read the entire article).

Marty retired from the Victor McLaglen Motor Corps at the ripe old age of 34 when Honda relocated him to Bozeman, Montana (in 2008) to serve as the District Sales Manager for the Honda motorcycle dealers. The regions he covered were Montana, North and South Dakota, and Wyoming. Marty married Allison Star and he whisked her away to live in Bozeman. The winters are, well, a bit wintry and a couple years later little Joshua Joseph Fisher was born.

After about four years in Montana, Honda decided to move the family to Pennsylvania. That lasted about a year before Honda returned them to California. Even though Marty was back in California, he had way too much going on in his life to devote much time to the Motor Corps. When there was a big, important show and the Corps was calling for some of their best riders to help out, he participated. But, that was just a once-in-a-while happening. It's too bad because he is an excellent rider; has superb management skills; is definitely a "people person;" and understands marketing, publicity and showmanship (so boasts his mom!). However, family comes first and his son, Josh, is immersed in school activities, soccer, baseball, ice hockey, birthday parties, and all those other things kids do nowadays. Marty is busy with the family (as he should be), but maybe someday there'll be a Fisher father-son duo on the team again. Josh already likes riding on the motorcycle with his dad, so there's hope!

"Front Fender Ride"
Motor Corps practice
2018
Marty & Josh (7 yrs old)

"Slow Circles"
Motor Corps practice
2019
Marty & Josh (8 yrs old)

Yep! I see a budding Motor Corps member growing up!

FISHER, RUTH H

As the wife of Harry Fisher, the leader and manager for the team, you might imagine how often and how many tasks I "volunteered" to do in order to support the Motor Corps.

It started when I offered to create and type the monthly schedules so the guys would know what was planned. I, then, discovered we really did need a good address and phone list for the members so they could keep in touch with one another. Next, Harry needed some articles written for the newspapers, flyers and programs for the shows, parade applications, etc.

Ruth Fisher
VMMC Announcer

Yes, you guessed it. My "volunteer" list continued until I was accomplishing practically all of the paperwork. This, of course, led to me coordinating the events and, when we performed away from home, scheduling motel/hotel and airplane reservations and any other travel arrangements that might be required.

Before the days of E-tickets for airline travel, we (I) held onto a stack of paper tickets. Because I just knew someone was bound to forget (or lose) their ticket, I would take all the tickets with me and distribute them at the airport. I also knew there was a good possibility some of the members might forget their uniforms (or they could be lost by the airlines), so I made sure all members packed their uniforms in plastic buckets which were loaded on a truck alongside their motorcycles. This ensured the uniforms also arrived at the show site. I also made sure that each member took only carry-on personal luggage. And, I was in charge of where we would stay, who doubled up with whom at the motel/hotel, when and where we would meet to unload the truck, when and where we would meet for each of the shows, and when and where we would eat and sleep, etc. It was a fun job and I did it for many years.

Just when I thought I had enough "volunteer" projects to keep me busy with the Motor Corps (after all, I also had a full-time job at McDonnell Douglas/Boeing), I was coerced into becoming the team announcer. It was 1992 and we were performing at the Sturgis Rally. The scheduled professional announcer was unable to make the trip and the team needed a replacement. I happened to be standing in the wrong place at the wrong time when Harry made eye contact with me! Yep, you guessed it. Beginning with Sturgis, I announced shows for the next 22 years.

I was genuinely surprised when I was granted a Life Membership with the Victor McLaglen Motor Corps at our Awards Banquet in 2014. The Corps had voted and I was a lifetime member. This was sneaky, too, since I was the one making all the banquet plans! However, this is an honor I cherish.

Ruth Fisher with
Corps Members (background)

FISK, NEWTON FRANKLIN

Newton became a member on February 9, 1957 and quit on June 10, 1958.

FITZGERALD, WAYNE (WAYNE)

In the early years (1935-1939), Wayne served as 1st Lieutenant and, according to Hap Ruggles, he was Captain DeRush's right-hand man. Outside of the Corps, Wayne worked as a distributor for electrical goods.

His name is engraved on the World Championship Trophy.

"Up on the Second Story"
Motorman: Wayne Fitzgerald
Top: Hap Ruggles

Motorman: Wayne Fitzgerald
Center Top: Hap Ruggles
Right Top: Jimmy Crawford
Left Top: Ernie Aguirre

Did you notice?
Stuntmen are hanging by their knees, one laying flat on the top (on an 11-foot high, 1-1/4" pipe) How the HECK do you drive and maneuver a vehicle like that?

FREEMAN, LLOYD GEORGE

Lloyd was voted in on August 8, 1953. Professionally, he worked for California Walnut Grocers.

FREEMAN, RALPH E

Ralph became a member on February 21, 1956 and quit on November 13, 1957.

FRENCH, GENE

Gene was one of the members who was voted in during the reorganization on April 2, 1978. He was a former member of the Huntington Park Elks Motorcycle Stunt and Drill Team before he "defected" to the Motor Corps. He quit in 1981.

Gene on the "High Pyramid"

"P-38 Ladder Headstand"
Gene French

Gene

FROST, KENNETH P (KENNY)

Kenny was voted into membership on October 27, 1964 and quit on December 1, 1967. He reapplied on November 3, 1991; was voted into membership (for the second time) on November 24, 1991; and quit again in 1992.

Kenny's Motor Corps bike was a 1972 Harley. He drove a big-rig truck and also owned a motorcycle funeral escort service.

Kenny Frost

FRYMOYER, KEN (KENNY)

Kenny applied for membership on November 13, 1984. Before an official vote was taken, he relocated to the East Coast. This move, however, put him in the right place at right time. During the New York City leg of their International Motorcycle Shows (IMS) tour, Kenny came to the rescue. He helped Harry Fisher and Tex Harris unload the motorcycles and equipment, then helped perform some entertaining stunts for the television cameras until the rest of the team arrived from the airport. Kenny was there when the team really needed him. Everyone was glad Kenny lived on the East Coast because the Corps was in a bind and his willingness to be there and help out was very much appreciated.

> Note: The slip clutch is also known as a rocker clutch where your whole foot is on the device and you rock it to engage or disengage the clutch. It is also known as a heel clutch, since it's operated just by your heel. When you load a bunch of people on your bike, the less you use the clutch, the smoother the ride. Jerky movements can be dangerous.

FRYMOYER, KIRBY U

Kirby was voted in on April 2, 1978 during the period when the Corps was going through a new reorganization. At the time, he worked with Harry Fisher at Hadley Auto Transport in Pico Rivera, California as a truck driver. He retired in 1995.

Kirby always considered himself to be a "Pennsylvania farm boy," and stated he bought his first motorcycle when he was 18 years old. It was a 1941 Harley and he rode it for nearly two years until the bottom end blew. Later, he bought a 1947 Harley and rode it until he enlisted in the Air Force in September of 1956. In 1958, while on home leave to Pennsylvania, Kirby purchased a 1954 Harley and rode this bike to Southern California where he was stationed at March Air Force Base in Riverside. It is

Kirby Frymoyer

interesting to note that the trip – from Pennsylvania to Riverside, California -- cost him a whopping $38.37.

In March of 1972, Kirby met Commander Harry Fisher, who invited him to a Motor Corps practice at the Huntington Park Elks. Kirby stated, "*I was so impressed, I joined immediately. Harry found a 1956 Harley for sale, which I bought, and he rode it home for me, so I could use it to ride in the team. I hadn't ridden since 1960, so was feeling a little too rusty for me to ride it home safely.*"

Kirby remembered when Harry switched from the Huntington Park Elks Motorcycle Stunt and Drill Team to the Victor McLaglen Motor Corps in 1978, he transitioned with him. The only difference was -- this time -- he brought his son, Mark. While discussing his time with the team and his son, Kirby said, "*It was a great honor to ride with my son in the world famous Victor McLaglen Motor Corps and I enjoyed every minute of it.*"

Thanks, Kirby, for all your support through the years. We've all enjoyed riding with you, too. Unfortunately for us, Kirby passed away in 2020.

FRYMOYER, MARK A

Mark is Kirby's son, and perhaps one of the most talented and dedicated riders on the team. Mark first began his passion for motorcycling at about age 10 when his father, Kirby, took him to the desert. It was there that he cultivated his skills. As he grew older and bigger, so did his bikes. His motorcycles not only got bigger, but they became more powerful. At age 15, Mark joined the team to ride with his dad.

"One-Legged Ride"

Mark Frymoyer

"Heisman"

FRYMOYER, MARK (Cont'd)

In addition to his membership with the Corps, there was a period of time when Mark worked as a Funeral Motorcycle Escort. A story written in the *Tax American Gearbox* magazine stated, "*It seems that one day, a couple of the men got stuck behind a long funeral procession. When their boredom reached its peak, they performed a couple of practice stunts right there in front of the funeral chapel. Just as the funeral party was exiting the chapel, one of the men in the Corps was sailing up the street standing backward on the seat and riding without using his hands on the throttle. The funeral director described everyone as being in a state of shock – everyone except the kids present, who started jumping up and down and screaming, "Neat! Neat!"* I'm not saying Mark was the individual doing that crazy stunt, but …

And, the stories don't stop there. There was time when the Corps was performing for the American Honda Motor Company's "Ride for Kids" event. This is an annual event that raises funds for Pediatric Brain Tumor children, and the team loves to do this show and mingle with the kids. Honda graciously loaned the team brand new Honda motorcycles, so they could have some of the "Kids" join them on the ride. I'm not exactly sure what happened; I heard something about wheelies. I'm guessing Mark got bored again! When he got bored, strange things happened. It's interesting to note that Honda didn't offer their bikes to us the following year.

Mark could ride any which way on his bike. Perhaps his most popular one-man stunt was the "Heisman Ride." It's simple. Just put one foot on the front fender, the other foot on the seat, balance your body on the left handlebar, and hold your arms out like you're flying. There's nothing to it! I do not know anyone who can (or would) do this stunt!

On April 2, 1978, Mark was accepted into the Motor Corps and he remains a loyal and enthusiastic member today. In fact, in 2018, he took over as our leader.

"Pivot Slow Circle"
Motorman: Mark Frymoyer
Seat: Janice Burgin
Right: James Burgin
Front Axle: Sue Hutchings

Although Mark excelled as a solo-stunt man, he also participated in many of the multiple stunts.

Mark said he was glad he joined the Corps with his dad. They were able to ride together for several years.

FRYMOYER, MARK A (Cont'd)

Mark enjoyed performing the two-man stunt known as "The Horse." For the grand finale, Mark (while standing on the shoulders of his motorman) would place the rope in his teeth and then extend both arms horizontally. This occurred while the motorman was tasked with controlling the bike and keeping it stable.

Mark lives in Los Angeles and is the owner/operator of a mobile diesel truck repair business.

"Slow Circle"
Mark maneuvers the bike into a tight slow circle placing one foot on the seat and one foot on the floorboard

"Horse"
Top: Mark Frymoyer
Motorman: Rigo Soto

Mark "giving 5" to the fans

"Front Crash Bar Ride"
Mark on his 1974 FLH with a handshift

Mark Frymoyer

FUDGE, LEROY (ROY)

Roy joined the Corps on July 2, 1957 and was appointed the Sergeant-of-Arms on February 11, 1958; he quit on March 11, 1958. I'll bet there's a story in there somewhere.

Professionally, he was a woodworker.

GALUSHA, ROBERT (BOB)

Bob was voted into the membership on April 2, 1978 as part of the new reorganization. Originally, he was a member of the Huntington Park Elks team. However, he decided to follow Harry Fisher when he left to lead the Victor McLaglen Motor Corps.

Bob rode in the Flag Unit. He was a good member and was always a lot of fun. Bob quit around 1980.

GARNER, STAN

Little information was found about Stan's membership, except that he more than likely participated during the early days, 1936-1939.

GARZA, GEORGE M (GEORGE)

George applied for membership on October 17, 1982 and rode with the team in the Flag Unit.

GEORGESON, LESLIE (Les)

Les became a member on July 23, 1963 and resigned in 1974.

He served as Club Treasurer in 1968, Vice President in 1969, President in 1970, and Executive-Board member in 1973.

Les Georgeson

Created by Tedd Farrell

GERRY, RICHARD D (DICK)

Dick was first voted into the Corps on September 17, 1957 and he first quit on December 31, 1965.

He could not, however, stay away and returned on September 17, 1978. Of course, what option did he have but to join again when Harry took charge? People are guessing that it also might have had something to do with Harry showing up at Dick's house late at night, riding his motorcycle onto the lawn, tipping over the trash cans, and revving the motor. Dick was not impressed with Harry's escapade as he was watching one of his favorite nighttime television shows (Chips?). He rose from his easy chair and opened the door to hear Harry shouting, "*You gotta get away from that TV and come back to ride with us! We're getting the team going and we need you.*" Well, I understand Dick's wife wasn't too pleased with the shenanigans in her front yard. Dick, on the other hand, must have thought it was pretty interesting because the next thing we knew, Dick Gerry was at the practice field … ready to ride!

During his 33 years with the Victor McLaglen Motor Corps, Dick participated as a motorman and stunt climber, and held numerous officer positions. He remained a dedicated member and an integral part of the team until his passing on February 25, 2000 when he was 78 years old. It is interesting to note that he also worked as a funeral escort motorcycle rider. Ironically, he was Escort Motor #78, and he rode his motorcycle until the last couple of weeks of his life. When Victor McLaglen passed away in 1959, Dick was asked by Mrs. McLaglen to be one of the pallbearers. Dick, of course, was privileged to have been asked and he participated in the funeral.

Dick was a retired U.S. Postman.

"One-Legged Ride"
Dick Gerry

"Spread Eagle"
Motorman Left: Dick Gerry
Motorman Right: Sam Watson
Middle Man: Harry Fisher
On Ground: Tedd Farrell

Dick Gerry
Late 1950s

GIVENS, LEE

Lee was voted into membership on October 29, 1957 and quit on May, 13, 1958.

GRAEB, KEN

The Motor Corps invited Ken to join them for the 2006 Love Ride. Ken was an employee of McDonnell Douglas Aircraft (MDC) and worked as a professional photographer for the company. We were performing and thought he could take some photographs of the team.

In addition to being a photographer, Ken was also an avid biker and he thoroughly enjoyed himself on the Love Ride. We decided, therefore, to ask him to consider applying for membership. There was, however, a major issue. Ken had a beard and the Bylaws required all teammates to be clean shaven. Ken wanted to join, the members wanted him to join … but, Ken wasn't about to shave off his beard.

So, what to do? The Corps found an easy fix. They merely changed the Bylaws and got with the times. Ken accepted our invitation, completed his application and was accepted by the membership on July 8, 2007. Unfortunately, shortly thereafter, he had to quit due to his retirement from MDC/The Boeing Company and a relocation to his new home in New Mexico.

"Speedo"
Left: Who is that Bearded Man?
Right: Mark Frymoyer

Ken Graeb, the photographer

Ken, the rider

GREEN, ERNEST RAY (RAY)

Ray was voted in on May 31, 1966 and resigned on November 12, 1968.

Ray rode a 1964 Harley and his wife, Doris, had a 1974 Harley. She attended practices with the team and he asked if Doris could ride with the Flag Unit. There is no evidence, however, that she actually performed at any of the shows.

Professionally, Ray worked as a carpenter.

"Horse"
Top: Ray Green
Motorman: Herb Harker

GREENWOOD, JOHN

Our best guess is that John was a member of the team from the late 1940s through the 1960s.

John was a Police Officer in Glendale, California.

GRIEST, RONNIE

Ronnie was voted into membership on November 6, 1954. He served as Acting Club Secretary in 1968 and graduated to a full-fledged Secretary in 1969.

Ronnie owned a cabin in Big Bear where the team occasionally got together for meetings. It was an especially nice place to stay and relax after they performed at the Big Bear Old Miner's Day Parade.

Banquet Time!
(L-R) Don Snow, Cliff Hamer, Ronnie Griest, Les Georgeson, Herb Harker

In 1936, the wives and girlfriends of members formed the "Auxiliary." After the Friday evening drill practice, they would serve coffee, pie, sandwiches, etc. for a social time. They wore matching uniforms and did what they could to support the team. Their uniformity helped the team win awards for "Most Members" contests at motorcycling events.

Here, Mary Militello presents a trophy to Ruth E. Fisher (Harry's mom) at the annual banquet. Ruth is wearing the official Auxiliary uniform which is black slacks and uniform shirt and tie. It's nearly identical to the official Motor Corps Class A uniform. Class B is with riding britches, helmet and tall boots.

The Auxiliary disbanded in 1984 as an official group but the wives and girlfriends continued to be the team's best supporters.

GRIFFIN, DEVIN

Devin was voted into membership on August 10, 2003. At the young age of 12, he was the youngest member ever! Although the bylaws did not accept members of Devin's age and members had to -- at the least -- have a driver's license and a motorcycle, an exception was made because Devin was the son of a current member, Scott Griffin.

As it turned out, the Anaheim-Fullerton Harley-Davidson gave the VMMC a promotional gift, the Whizzer. It was decided that Devin would ride the new Harley-Davidson Whizzer at the shows.

Devin was a good sport and a welcomed addition to the team. Unfortunately, Devin had to quit and do school things.

Scott kickstarts Devin's Whizzer

Devin Griffin

"Chariot Ride" Devin Griffin

GRIFFIN, SCOTT

Scott joined the team on March 17, 2002. He began as a safetyman, but eventually transitioned into the motorman position for the High Pyramid, as well as performing several solo stunts. With more than ten years of riding experience with the VMMC, Scott progressed into a solid, reliable member. When Colonel Fisher suddenly passed in 2014, Scott took charge and let the members know he wanted to carry on what Harry had started. The membership voted and he was accepted as the new Commander and Drill Leader. Scott continued to do an excellent job until he resigned four years later. It's not easy being the fourth leader of the oldest motorcycle stunt and drill team in the world.

"Floorboard Ride"

"One Motor Pyramid"
Safety: Scott Griffin
Top: Mickey Minor
Middle: Moe Elmoe
Motorman: Mike Betschart

Scott posing on his 1970 Harley FLH

GRIFFINS, PAUL E
Paul was voted into membership on September 26, 1959 and quit on March 22, 1960. He rode a 1949 Harley and, when he wasn't riding his bike, worked as a Machine Operator.

GRIGGS, CHARLES
Charles joined the team in the 1940s.
The photo shows Charles in the front, lay-back position of the "Sunflower."

"Sunflower"
Charles Griggs on front

HALL, NATE
Nate became a member on September 14, 1978 and quit the VMMC about a year later.

HAMER, CLIFTON J (CLIFF)
Cliff was voted into membership on February 7, 1961, served as Secretary and remained until June 27, 1967. Cliff rode a 1955 black and white Harley and worked professionally as a truck driver. He sold his 1933 Harley to Harry Fisher.

Right: Cliff accepts
Secretary gavel
Left: Colonel Harker

Cliff Hamer

Harry Fisher shows
off Cliff's 1933 Harley
(purchased later)

HAMMACK, DELMAR
Delmar joined the team on August 29, 1961 and quit on March 29, 1962. He rode a 1959 Harley and worked as a truck driver.

HANCOCK, ALBERT RICHARD
Albert was voted in on December 4, 1962 and quit on September 9, 1963. He rode a 1951 Harley.

HARDIN, HARRY D

Harry was voted in on July 6, 1954, was elected President in 1956 and quit on November 26, 1957. (It must've been a tough job!)

HARKER, WILLIAM HERBERT (HERB)

Herb was the second leader in the Motor Corps assuming the reins from Captain DeRush. He joined the team on August 4, 1953 and led the team until 1978 when Harry Fisher accepted the leadership role.

William Herbert (Herb) Harker was born in Chicago, Illinois on May 8, 1919 and his birth certificate was actually signed by Governor Frank O. Lowden.

Herb & Liz 1940   *Herb retired from the team in 1978*

Herb was adopted by Paul and Margaret Harker in 1920. He was just 1½ years old when his adoptive parents took a train ride to Chicago to pick him up and take him to live on their farm in Elmwood, Illinois.

Herb purchased his first motorcycle – a 1930 Harley 74 – in Galesburg, Illinois in 1932; he was almost 14 years old. In 1936, Herb met Elizabeth (Liz). It was a blind date and it was Liz's first motorcycle ride. Liz stated she never felt she could handle riding a motorcycle by herself; she just enjoyed riding behind Herb.

In the early 1940s, Herb ventured to California where he attended the Anderson Aircraft School. After accepting a job at Lockheed Aircraft Corporation in Burbank, he figured it was a good time to ask Liz to come to Los Angeles to be his bride. They were married on September 27, 1940 and their son, Richard, was born in 1944.

Herb worked for Douglas Aircraft Company (DAC) until 1950 when he started escorting funerals for Hap Ruggles and Frank Ketter. It just so happened Hap had been a key man in the Victor McLaglen Motor Corps.

See the connection now?

Herb & Liz

HARKER, HERB (Cont'd)

In 1953, Herb was the owner of Pico Harley-Davidson in Montebello, California. In 1960, Herb returned to escorting funerals on his motorcycle for Ronnie Griest's funeral escort business. Ronnie was also a Motor Corps member. When Ronnie died in 1970, Herb bought the escort business and renamed it Harker's Escort Service. I don't know what happened to Pico Harley-Davidson.

It was his exceptional leadership skills and excellent riding abilities, as well as the endless respect he earned from the entire membership, which enabled Herb to hold the team together for more than 25 years. The VMMC team felt a very special bond and much appreciation for the dedication and love exhibited by Herb and Liz. They will always be remembered for their devotion and loyalty to the Motor Corps.

In 1978, as Herb's health began to fail, he sold his funeral motorcycle escort business to Al Blomker, owner of Secure Funeral Escort Service, and Herb and Liz moved to Oregon. Their final move took place in 1992 when Herb returned to Fairview, Illinois where he passed away on August 17, 1992.

1968 Annual Banquet

"Rear Handstand" Motorman Herb with Mike Catford 1969

"Seat Stand" Herb 1971

Motorman Herb

Herb, Liz & the Corps 1973 Clay Canyon Run

Herb & Liz

HARRIS, ROBERT M (TEX)

Tex joined the team on October 29, 1995. He worked as a truck driver and, when the team performed their first tour with the Indoor Motorcycle Shows (IMS), he and Harry Fisher "team-drove" the big 18-wheeler. Their journey was exhausting and the schedule demanding; however, it didn't stop Tex and Harry from ensuring the stunt bikes and equipment arrived safe and sound. And, or course, Harry and Tex also performed in the shows.

They departed Long Beach and their first two stops were in San Mateo, California and Seattle, Washington. A horrendous snowstorm followed them to Fargo, North Dakota and Chicago, Illinois. It was in Cleveland, Ohio that their show was canceled because the Fire Marshall would not allow the motorcycles into the convention hall. This didn't stop'em, though! The truck drove onward to performances in New York City; Pontiac, Michigan; Minneapolis, Minnesota; and, finally, Denver, Colorado before heading home to California.

In addition to being a terrific trucker, Tex was a super safetyman.

1995 International Motorcycle Shows (IMS) Truck Travel Route

HASEROT, LES

Les joined in 1937 and stayed with the team for a couple of years. One of Les's stunts involved riding his motorcycle through a burning wood tunnel structure; successfully, we think!

Les's name is engraved on the World Championship Trophy. It's interesting to note that Les was a former member of the Barnum and Bailey Circus show as a metrodome and loop-the-loop rider.

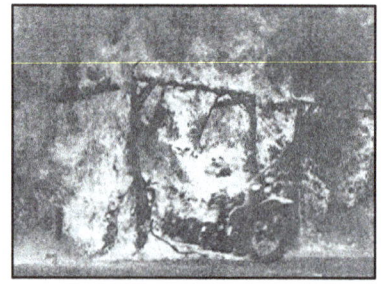

"Fire Tunnel"

Front: Les Haserot
Motorman: Hap Ruggles
Back: John Crawford

HICKS, FRANCIS J (FATHER FRANK)

Frank became a Victor McLaglen Motor Corps (VMMC) member on April 27, 1980 and he remains active today. Frank reminisces about his history with the Corps. I think you'll enjoy reading some of his memories below and also better understand how he came to be one of the Corps most valued members.

My first contact with the Motor Corps was in an article I read in Motorcycling Magazine some time in 1963. It featured a very young Harry Fisher doing the spread eagle and a somewhat older Dick Gerry doing the push-up chariot. It was phenomenal. Of course, I was still living on the east coast and participation with the Motor Corps wasn't even on the horizon. What lay ahead was graduate school, the Peace Corps in Thailand (my first motorcycle, a Honda) and, in 1972, a transfer from the Border Patrol in West Texas to Criminal Investigation here in Southern California, home of the VMMC.

I was riding, I believe at that time, a Yamaha Xcel II and I joined the SCMA. The Motor Corps had a charter membership with the SCMA, so I got a renewed and close-up look at the Corps. I liked what I saw, submitted my application to the Motor Corps and attended the requisite practices in the parking lot on Pixie Ave. in Long Beach; I think it was at the Aviation Workers Union Headquarters.

I was voted on as a rookie and my first Harley was a black and white, brand spanking new late 1978 or '79 FLH 80 which is still in the Corps. It came out the door from Brian Shiffenmiller's (sic) Upland Harley-Davidson for $4922. Those were the days. I started in the Flags Unit, but also participated in drill and stunts; particularly the pyramid (seat man), push-up chariot (push-up safety) and many of the smaller stunts. Member Chuck Buckner was a great teacher."

Motorman: Sam Watson
Motorman: Harry Fisher
Safetyman: Fr. Frank

In the day, we led about 15 to 20 parades and at least a dozen shows each year. When we weren't doing shows, we were practicing at the Huntington Park Elks Lodge parking lot. I participated in the United States Jamboree in Ventura where we put 22 men on one motorcycle and just about all the shows and parades during that time. Most of our shows were in the immediate area of Los Angeles, but we did also perform at Yuma, Arizona for the Yuma Prison Run and at the Santa Maria Rodeo Parade.

Fr. Frank presents the American Flag at a show

HICKS, FRANCIS J (FATHER FRANK) (Cont'd)

In 1980, we did shows for the Aspencade Run in New Mexico. What a project that was; two weeks just getting the truck loaded with all the bikes, transporting them to Ruidoso, New Mexico, unloading and parking for the event, then loading back up, transporting them back to California, and unloading again, say nothing of getting the Motor Corps members to the airports and flying them there and back.

In 1984, we performed in Reno, Nevada and had a great time. I remember Larry Castro riding on my '33 which was transported in the back of Bruce Chubbuck's pick-up truck. We drove through Reno and were stopped by a cop for unsafe riding practices. I think the motor cop wanted a close up look at the '33 and we did not get a ticket ... Then I can remember Harry just about losing the beer he was drinking when Bob Holbrook announced that he did not like his room assignment. He wanted to sleep with Frank Hicks (figuratively only – share a room would have been much better wording. Those were great years and I had a lot of fun. It was hard work and a lot of time, but worth it all.

The Motor Corps has persevered because it is something worth keeping in our finest American tradition. Though other countries may have government-sponsored groups, we survived and flourished because of a group of men and women who believe it is worth the effort, time, and treasure to preserve and keep such a great institution as the Victor McLaglen Motor Corps. God Bless the VMMC."

Frank was ordained to the priesthood in Los Angeles by Cardinal Roger Mahoney in 2000 and began his journey as a Catholic priest. In 2006, Frank was installed as the Pastor of St. Basil's Catholic Church in Los Angeles and also served as Chaplain of both the Los Angeles Police and Fire Departments.

Frank arrives at practice after conducting early Mass

Today, Father Frank serves as the chaplain of the Victor McLaglen Motor Corps. When Harry Fisher died, Father Frank was there to conduct the funeral service. It was a very difficult job because of their close friendship.

Father Frank has since conducted funeral services for several more of our members.

Father Frank also officiated the special memorial to place an engraved marker at the gravesite of Captain Truman (Nick) Ward DeRush at Inglewood Park Cemetery in March 2022. This had been an unmarked grave since Nick passed away in 1962. (See Appendix F)

Frank Hicks Chaplain

Father Frank's hobbies include motorcycling (Harley-Davidsons, of course), music, reading, stamp collecting, traveling, cooking, raising orchids and gardening in general. (See Appendix G)

HICKS, TYLOR

Tylor was first voted in on June 10, 1969. He was 19 and, due to the VMMC Bylaws at that time, he couldn't join until he received permission from his parents. He was in and out of the team several times before moving to Colorado. When he returned to California, he joined the team once again in 1979 (during the reorganization).

Tylor Hicks on his 1988 FLHS

Tylor had purchased a new 1978 Harley and he was ready to ride. This time, his stint with the team lasted almost 10 years before he had to resign. In 1997, he came to a practice session and participated in a few stunts. Harry mentioned that he could always re-join and that's exactly what Tylor did. Within a couple of years, he'd bought a 1988 Harley FLHS and he remained with the team until his retirement in 2015. Tylor was a loyal supporter of the Motor Corps, helping with administration duties, as well as doing his part in the stunts and drill riding. He delighted the crowds when he did the "sweeper" position on the DC-10, dragging his shirt on the pavement.

"High Pyramid"

"DC-10"
Tylor Hicks
Sweeper position on back

(L-R): Marty Fisher, Jake Elmore, Tylor Hicks, Sue Hutchings

HILL, MICHAEL M (MIKE)

Mike was the son of member, Dick Hill. He was voted into membership on June 9, 1985 at the age of 14. His application said he had been riding since he was five years old. Like his dad, Mike also rode a mini bike in the shows, and father and son remained members of the team for a couple of years.

HILL, RICHARD (DICK)

Dick was voted in on July 8, 1984. Although he was a big guy, he rode a mini bike, which was used for safety. The team's safetymen would ride alongside large and complicated stunts, such as the High Pyramid, to keep spectators out of the way. Dick performed as a safetyman, however his primary task was acting as announcer for the shows and handling publicity. He was a radio show host for a local radio program called "Center Stand," and a technical writer for motorcycle magazines, so he held a wealth of knowledge. Dick wrote articles for the Harley-Davidson Owners Association (H.D.O.A.) monthly newsletter, *The American Gearbox*. The H.D.O.A., founded by Carl and Cindy Wicks, was the forerunner of the Harley-Davidson Company's Harley Owners Group (H.O.G.).

Unfortunately, Dick was killed in 1987 when a homemade bomb was mailed to his home. Dick's son, Mike, brought in the package addressed to Dick, Dick opened it and it exploded. He died nine days later. The culprit was found and convicted of the crime and sentenced to 25 years to life.

Although Dick rode a mini-bike as a Safetyman, he liked the big bikes, too!

HOLBROOK, ROBERT (BOB)

Bob was voted in on May 18, 1980. He rode a 1976 black and white Harley, and remained with the team for about ten years.

Bob worked as a Data Processing Analyst for the Hughes Aircraft Company and was featured in an article in his company newspaper, the "EDSG," Electro-Optical & Data Systems Group, August 1981. (See Appendix H)

"High Pyramid"
Safetyman: Bob Holbrook
South Gate, California

HORN, FRANKLIN D R (FRANK)

Frank was voted into membership on December 13, 1961 and Resigned on January 9, 1968.

Frank Horn

HOWELL, CLAUDE R (CHUCK)

Chuck was a team member from 1937 through 1942 when he left For the service and WWII. Chuck rode a 1966 FLH Harley (pictured below). During the shows, you could often see Chuck pulling a little teardrop trailer (loaded with equipment) behind his stunt bike.

Chuck Howell tows Team Equipment Trailer

HUTCHINGS, SUE

Sue was the second female stunt and drill member ever admitted to the Motor Corps, so you know she had to have been a good rider! (Maria Willers was the first female member.)

It happened like this: Following a show in Irvine, California for the Children's Hospital of Orange County (CHOC), Sue approached Harry Fisher to discuss riding. She said she was trying to improve her riding skills and wanted some advice.

Sue Hutchings

Naturally, Harry invited Sue to come to a team practice, and that's all it took. She came to practice, Harry saw how well she could ride, had her participate in a bit of drill riding, put her on a stunt, and handed her an application!

Sue was voted in on November 3, 2002 after MUCH scrutiny from the guys in the team. After all, she was a *woman* applicant, you know. Sue improved her riding skills and improved the teams' shows. Yay for *woman power*!

"Riding in Pairs"
Art Wales &
Sue Hutchings

"P-38"
Maria Willers: Left
Sam Watson: Center
Sue Hutchings: Right
Mike Betschart: Motorman

"Front Fender Layback"
Sue Hutchings: Front Fender
Scott Griffin: Motorman

IRVING, NEIL

Neil joined the team on November 13, 1956. He rode a 1956 Harley, and Harry Fisher once told him he was the best slow-circle rider he knew. Neil said it was pretty simple and he didn't understand what the big deal was. Neil also donated his truck service to the club members when needed to pick up an ailing bike, which was always appreciated. From 1957 through 1959, he served as Vice President. On April 24, 1962, he wrote a letter stating he didn't have enough time to devote to being a good member. The December 10, 1963 meeting minutes showed his request was met and he was placed on the "Inactive List."

JAMES, NEIL

Neil was voted in on February 1958 at the age of 59. He worked as a writer at Republic Studios, a motion picture production company in California.

JACKSON, JERRY

Jerry was voted in on November 11, 1979 and he rode in the Flag Unit.

JENSON, ROBERT (BOB)

Bob joined the membership on August 27, 1978. Bob was a strong, steady motorman, and the guys could always depend on him to keep the stunt going smoothly and up on two wheels. Bob did not have the use of his right eye and often wore a patch. It didn't seem to bother him too much when he was riding his bike. In fact, the team often forgot he had a vision handicap.

Bob Jenson

After 23 years with the Motor Corps and a number of years previously with the Huntington Park Elks Motorcycle Stunt and Drill Team, Bob was one of the more experienced and valuable riders. His wife, Evelyn, was the Motor Corps photographer for many of those years and was often seen toting her camera at one of the shows.

Bob worked as a heavy equipment operator for many years and, when he quit working in 2001, he also retired from the Motor Corp.

Bob Jenson & his Bike

Bob & his Wife, Evelyn

"Horse"
Motorman: Bob Jensen
Standing: Dan Welch

JERNIGAN, JAMES (JIM)

Jim was voted in on May 31, 1960 and quit on April 12, 1962. He rode a 1956 Harley and worked as a funeral escort officer.

JESTER, HARLAN

Harlan was originally a member of the Victor McLaglen Light Horse Drill Team. It was during this time that he met Grace, his bride-to-be. In 1936, he joined the VMMC team to impress her even more!

JOHNSON, LARRY

Larry joined the team on July 24, 1983 and participated as a motorman until 1985.

Motorman: Harlan Jester
Rear: Jim Underwood

JONES, MICKEY (HONORARY MEMBER 2014)

Mickey was an actor and musician who took an interest in the Motor Corps when he was hosting one of their shows. Mickey had played drums with the bands of Bob Dylan, Trini Lopez, Johnny Rivers, and Kenny Rogers. When he transitioned to acting, he played roles in "National Lampoon's Vacation" and "Total Recall" (with Arnold Schwarznegger). He was the character, Rodney 'Hot Rod' Durham, in "Justified," and became one of the well-recognized construction workers on Tim Allen's "Home Improvement" television series.

Mickey was so impressed with the Motor Corps that he produced a documentary movie for us in 2012. It was excellent. He was a great advocate of the Motor Corps and always added greatness to our shows whenever he attended.

Mickey passed away in 2018, four years after his "best bud," Harry Fisher, passed. Mickey made a beautiful video as a tribute to Harry's life that he showed at Harry's funeral and I know Harry would have done the same at Mickey's funeral if he could have. As it was, many of the current Motor Corps members attended Mickey's funeral and it was a sad day for all. Mickey is definitely missed.

Ruth & Mickey Jones
"Love Ride"

Harry Fisher & Mickey Jones

Mickey

KATTHOEFER, DENNIS

Dennis was voted in on April 2, 1978 and quit on May 16, 1979. He was a big guy; tall and strong, and a terrific safetyman.

KAZIAN, JOHN MARK (JOHNNY)

Johnny was voted in on February 11, 1964 and quit on March 8, 1965. Johnny and Harry Fisher were good buddies and often did things together. For instance, they "defected" from the VMMC to join the Huntington Park Elks Motorcycle Stunt and Drill Team. You might recall (in the Harry Fisher section of this book) that Johnny and Harry were also working on an act so they could run away and join the circus.

Harry's 1933 Harley (1966)
Motorman: Harry Fisher
Rear: Johnny Kazian

Following John's stint with motorcycle stunt driving, he transitioned to perform wing walking on a biplane, piloted by the legendary aerobatic pilot and International Council of Air Shows (ICAS) Hall of Fame member, Joe C. Hughes. John was also one of the first men in the world to hang at the end of a rope ladder (suspended from a plane) while he was pulled through a burning wall of fire. Another one of his stunts involved transferring from a speeding car to an airplane on that same ladder.

(See Appendix I)

Johnny crashing a firewall while suspended on a rope ladder

"Swan"
Top: Johnny Kazian

KELLER, ROBERT E (BOB)

Bob joined the Motor Corps on May 4, 1971. He redesigned the slip-clutch for the team to make it simpler and cheaper, and the Corps starting using his new device in 1979. Bob was part of the new reorganized team that took effect in 1978. He quit in 1981.

"Rear Rack Headstand"
Upside Down: Bob Keller
Motorman: Herb Harker

KELLEY, TOM

Tom was voted in on August 11, 1971, but left shortly thereafter on November 9, 1971.

KEMP, STANLEY

Stanley joined the team in 1948 when he was 18 years old. We heard from him in 2013, when he was 83 years old. He contacted us to see how the Motor Corps was doing.

KENYON, MIKE

Records show Mike was voted in on January 17, 1956. His official membership date, however, was documented as June 1, 1960. I think someone wasn't keeping track of things very well!

Mike Kenyon   *"Seat Stand"*
              Mike Kenyon

KERLEY, ROGER

Roger became a member of the Victor McLaglen Motor Corps in the late 1930s.

Roger Kerley (far left)

KLEIN, BOB

Klein's name is engraved on the World Championship Trophy. He was also a former member of the Barnum and Bailey Circus show as a metrodrome and loop-the-loop rider.

KOKOL, GILBERT (GIL)

Gil was voted in on January 5, 1960 and quit on July 1, 1960. Gil was a motorcycle Honor Guard at Victor McLaglen's funeral along with members Lyle Carmody, Dick Gerry and Ronnie Griest.

KREIDER, WILLIAM (BILL)

Bill joined in 1949 and I don't know how long he was active. He did, however, attend one of our shows in Sparks, Nevada in 2005. He rode his restored 1925 JE Harley to the staging area and let the team ride it around a bit.

Bill shared one of his stories. "*We once put on a show at the old Culver City Raceway. We were doing the stunt with all the guys on one motor and Phil Erickson on his bike. Suddenly, we hit a bad bump in front of the grandstands and we all just about fell off. Phil let out a big moan but we kept going to our staging area. When we stopped, we found out Phil had broken his back; but, by God, he finished the show.*" This is just another example of "the show must go on" attitude that was shared by all the Corps members.

By 1954, Bill had finished college and accepted a position in the motorcycle division for the Los Angeles Police Department. After twenty years with the department, he retired.

In 2002, at the age of 85, Bill joined the Military Vehicle Preservation Association on a 4000-mile roundtrip convoy to Alaska. He rode his 1942 WLA (which is a Harley 45cu) which he had personally restored. This bike was a replicate of the one he rode in Germany at the end of World War II when he served with the 1st Infantry Division Military Police.

KULT, RAYMOND (RAY)

Ray joined the team on August 16, 1992. Although he didn't own a motorcycle, his superb balance and coordination made climbing to the top of the Pyramid and doing handstands on the side of the bikes look simple.

Ray had previously worked as a professional skateboarder putting on exhibitions along with

"Ladder Ride"
Ladder: Ray Kult
Motorman: Harry Fisher

"High Pyramid"
Top: Ray Kult

his pal, Johnny Walker, who joined the Motor Corps at the same time. Both men were phenomenal.

KURI, COLONEL ADOLPH (COLONEL KURI)

My understanding is that although Colonel Kuri was not an official member of the Motor Corps, he was very much involved with the team. As Victor McLaglen's business manager, he dealt with the business end of things from the early days up through the 1960s when he oversaw the team operations for Mrs. McLaglen after Victor's passing. Colonel Kuri attended several meetings, banquets and shows throughout the years and was instrumental in acquiring venues where the team could perform.

LATCHAT, CARMEN

Carmen was voted in on November 5, 1974 and rode a 1970 Harley. In 1976, he was promoted to Sergeant but dropped out that same year.

LATZ, JAY R

Jay and his 1956 Harley joined the team on December 19, 1961. He was, however, removed from the rolls "due to lack of attendance" on February 12, 1963 (per the meeting minutes). On November 1, 1963, he was killed in an airplane accident near Riverside, California.

LAUERS, ROBERT WAYNE (BOB)

Bob was voted on to the team on May 19, 1981 where he performed as a mini-bike safety rider.

LAUSCHE, DENNIS

Dennis joined the VMMC in 1979 after leaving the Huntington Park Elks Motorcycle Stunt and Drill Team.

LEE, TROY

Troy joined the team on October 21, 1993 as a mini-bike safety rider.

Troy had a colorful past. Prior to his retirement as an aerospace special response mechanic at McDonnell Douglas Corporation in Long Beach, he had been a professional motorcycle racer. He raced at the old Ascot Raceway in Gardena, California and even defeated Sammy Tanner, "The Flying Flea," before going on to win the 1960 Springfield Mile race. The founder of Troy Lee Designs was named after "our" Troy Lee!

Picture taken from Troy Lee Designs website

LOCKE, OTTO

Otto performed with the team in the late 1940s. When he was in his 80s, he attended several of the Annual Yuma Prison Runs in Yuma, Arizona. He had an entertaining personality and it was always a treat to talk with him.

LOMAS, BILL and RONNIE (HONORARY MEMBERS)
Bill and Ronnie owned Pageantry Productions in Lynwood, California and invited the Motor Corps to lead many of their local parades (1979 through the 1980s).

LOWER, BOB
Bob joined the team on May 10, 1982 and quit in 1982.

MACIAS, AL
Al was originally a member of the Huntington Park Elks until he joined the VMMC on May 11, 1980; he quit about 1985.

MAINE, EARL B
Earl was voted in on November 12, 1967. He served as Recording Secretary in 1968 and resigned in 1970 after serving as the club's Vice President.

MANSHARDT, RALPH
Ralph's name is engraved on the World Championship Trophy. Ralph rode with the team until he enlisted in the U.S. Army in 1942. After returning home, Ralph worked in Los Angeles at Rapid Blue Print where he met Harry Fisher. Their friendship at work developed because of their shared connection with the Motor Corps.

The World Championship trophy was awarded to members of the Victor McLaglen Motor Corps in 1935. Since then, it passed from one person to another and, along the way, one of the side motorcycles (see photo) was lost. Later, Tom Scott, Fullerton Harley-Davidson, had the trophy restored. The remaining motorcycle was placed on the top. The eagle took its original position and another eagle was added to the other side to create balance. The trophy remained on display in Tom's shop for several years before being moved to California Harley-Davidson in Harbor City, CA

Names of the VMMC contest participants are engraved on the five plates (see bottom front).

MANURI, SALVATORE (SAL)

Sal joined the team in the 1950s and quit when he returned to New Jersey.

His daughter wrote to me that he was in the Navy, was a Golden Glove Boxer, an auto mechanic, and an owner of two gas stations (Texaco & Sal's Sinclair) in Cranford, New Jersey.

She sent pictures of the team performing at a prison. The back of one of the pictures says, "Victor McGlaughlin (sic) Motor Corp Alcatraz," but I'm wondering if it is Alcatraz. Not only does it look like there just isn't a big enough cemented space on the island (as shown in the photo), but in order for the 20 bikes and men to get to Alcatraz, they would have had to be transported on a ferry. That would have been quite a feat. It would have been

Sal Manuri
1936 Harley Knucklehead

necessary to tie down all 16 motorcycles so they didn't fall over with all the rockin' and rollin' of the boat. Also, my research revealed that the warden at Alcatraz in the late 1940s and early 1950s was not well liked by either the prisoners or the staff. It seems unlikely that he would have allowed this type of entertainment at his prison. But, then, it does say "Alcatraz" on the back of the picture and it does look like they did one heck of a show, wherever it was. I'm going to call it San Quentin, though. I think that was most likely where this show took place. (See Appendix I)

1950 – Alcatraz or San Quentin Prison, California

Sal's in there somewhere!

MARGRAVES, STANLEY
Corporal Margraves' name is engraved on the World Championship Trophy and he rode with the team in the 1930s.

MARTIN, ALVIS R
Alvis joined the Motor Corps on April 5, 1981 and quit some time in 1985.

MARTIN, HENRY E (DOC)
Doc worked for the U.S. Navy, so he wrote on his application "*Cannot join Civil Defense. Belong to the U.S. Navy.*" There was no date or further information provided. Because his paperwork was signed by Herb Harker, we know his association with the Motor Corps had to have been in the 1950-1960s.

MARTIN, RON (RONNIE)
Ronnie was voted in on February 10, 1959.

MATHIS, ERNEST Z
Ernest joined on September 3, 1957 and quit on April 8, 1958. He worked as a truck driver.

MAY, GARY A
Records indicate Gary joined on March 31, 1964, went "Inactive" on July 1, 1964 then, finally, quit on August 1, 1964.

Gary worked as an exterminator and rode a 1960 Harley.

McCARTNEY, FRANK
Corporal McCartney rode with the team in the 1930s and his name is engraved on the World Championship Trophy.

Created by Tedd Farrell

McCOOL, RONALD B (RON)

Ron was voted in on October 24, 2010 and rode with the Flag Bearer Unit. He retired from Northrop Grumman in 2013 after 41 years of service.

McCLELLAN, GEORGE

George was accepted by the membership on September 6, 1964 and again on November 3, 1964. Why twice? I have no idea. He eventually quit in 1967 and moved to Virginia where he became a police officer.

Headstand: Mike Catford
Motorman: George McClellan

McDONALD, JOSEPH WILLIAM (BILL)

Bill was voted in on May 20, 1979. He assisted in negotiations for Motor Corps shows, which was very helpful. One such show was the 1979 SCMA Three Flags Classic. This motorcycle run began in Tijuana, Mexico and ended in Vancouver, Canada which entailed riding through three countries; Mexico, USA and Canada.

He also helped build the unique equipment required on the motorcycle for the "many-men-on-a-motorcycle" stunt which the team performed in Tijuana, Mexico. Unfortunately, the show ended in tragedy when the Tijuana Police Motorcycle Team staged a stunt which resulted in the death of one of their members and two other members severely injured.

We never knew it, but Bill had a serious heart problem and never should have been doing the stunts that he so loved. He passed away a year later at the early age of 42 years old.

MEHLBAUM, RAY

Ray was voted in on April 4,1993 and resigned on October 1, 2000. He was a true showman – performing for the crowds with a big smile and striving for perfection.

Ray was a business owner and he also worked as a motorcycle funeral escort.

Marty Fisher & Ray Mehlbaum

"Slow Circles"
Ray Mehlbaum

Yep ... the stunt flopped! It had to bomb in front of 20,000 people at the Love Ride, no less.
Ray ????? He thought it was pretty funny!

MEYERS, KELLY

It was in Oklahoma in the early 1930s when Kelly and two of his brothers jumped on their Harleys and headed to California. It wasn't long before Kelly got involved with the Motor Corps (probably 1937) and started doing tricks. Kelly was among six bikers who rode Indian motorcycles in 1941. His departure from VMMC also resulted in the end of riding Indian motorcycles on the team.

Kelly went on to make a name for himself as a racer. Eventually, he met racer, Ed Kretz, and began flat track racing. He was presented with an opportunity to own a motorcycle shop with Johnson Motors as his sponsor. He declined the offer and retired from racing in the early 50s.

"Double 1-Legged Ride"

Kelly Meyers

Kelly Meyers
1936 VL 74

After looking at the photographs of Kelly's motorcycle, our Motor Corps Harley expert, Bruce Chubbuck, stated, *"This was the last year for the VL 74 and the first year with 61 EL OHV. The front end is the same on the bike in both pictures but the handlebars have been reshaped."*

MILITELLO, JOSEPH (JOE)

Joe joined the Motor Corps on November 3, 1964. He was very active in helping to manage the team and held numerous positions including Sergeant of Arms (1968), Secretary (1969-1970), Stunt Leader (1971), and Vice President (1973).

"Swan"
Motorman: Joe Militello
Top: Mike Catford

Motorman: Joe Militello
From General Motors
Differential demonstration

"Sunflower"
Motorman: Joe Militello

MINOR, MELVIN W (MEL)

Mel joined the Flag Bearer unit of the Motor Corps on December 2, 2007.

Mel Minor with Motor Corps Flag

MINOR, MERIDETH (MICKEY)

(no relation to Mel Minor)

Following his retirement from the U.S. Navy, Mickey worked as an operations engineer for the University of California at Irvine (UCI). He retired from UCI, applied for membership with the Motor Corps, was voted in, and joined on May 5, 1985.

Mickey connected with the team to improve his riding skills. He wanted to control his ability to ride slower and turn tight corners. Overall, he just aspired to be a better rider. It wasn't too long before the members discovered Mickey had additional talents. At 148 lbs., and 5'9", he was lightweight, agile and strong. He was phenomenal and exactly what the team needed! He could climb on shoulders and stand easily, and he could do a handstand on the shoulders of two guys who were standing on a moving motorcycle.

From 1985 to 2010, Mickey was the top guy; literally! In fact, Mickey held the highest position on the High Pyramid - the TOP.

When he finally resigned from the team on January 2, 2010, he was 78 years old. In letting Harry know he was retiring, Mickey said, "*I just don't think I have the strength to do it right anymore.*"

I once asked him if he practiced or worked out. He responded in his great Arkansas drawl, "*Well, I do stand on my head some, next to the kitchen wall.*"

Mickey Minor

MINOR, MERIDETH (MICKEY) (Cont'd)

An interesting story I heard firsthand was when Mickey and Dan Welch were secretly practicing the stunt known as the *Wheelbarrow Ride*. Their secret was exposed when Mickey arrived at team practice with a broken rib. In fact, both he and Dan were pretty bruised. Harry asked, "*What happened to you guys?*" Mickey said, "*Well, it's like this. Me and Dan was trying to perfect that Wheelbarrow stunt and sorta tumbled off.*" Harry gave them a little all-important hint on what they were doing wrong and they finally got it right! This was also an opportunity for Harry to remind the members to practice **with** the team to ensure accidents did not occur and everyone remained safe.

"Wheelbarrow Ride"
Mickey (Upside down)
Dan Welch (Safety)

"1-Motor Pyramid"
Top: Mickey Minor

"High Pyramid"
Top: Mickey Minor

Mickey was born and raised in DeValls Bluff, Arkansas (2020 population = 510). Mickey agreed to share his motorcycle story. It is, of course, a good one! (See Appendix J)

Mickey on his 1984 Harley

Musical Entertainment
VMMC Banquet
Mickey Minor (Right)
Moe Elmore (Left)

Stunt Leader
Mickey Minor

> Question: What's the most dangerous part of a motorcycle?
> Answer: The nut that connects the seat to the handlebar.

MOHR, FROSTY
Frosty joined the team on August 29, 1978 and quit on December 23, 1979. He rode in the Flag Bearer Unit and worked as a motorcycle funeral escort.

MOORE, MICHAEL J (HOLLYWOOD)
Hollywood was voted on to the team on July 13, 2008.

Hollywood was quite a colorful character and much of his career involved performing specialty acts. In one such act, he was highlighted as "The Old Whipper Snapper" as he entertained his audience by cracking a bullwhip. Another act involved throwing knives at his partner who was strapped to a spinning wheel.

Hollywood restored an old Indian motorcycle. It looked like new and in perfect condition when he was finished. He also built a 1/10th scale replica of one of the Harley stunt bikes and rode it in some of the shows.

MORGAN, HOMER WILSON
When Homer was accepted as a member on March 17, 1959, he was riding a brand new 1959 Harley. He quit on June 23, 1959.

MORTON, HERBERT V
Herbert was a member prior to the 1950s. He was invited to be a special guest at the 1956 VMMC Banquet.

MORTON, KERMIT
Kermit was voted into membership on March 9, 1954. He worked for Pacific Union Metal Company.

MULDOON, PATRICK M
Patrick was voted on to the team on October 29, 1957 and dropped out on May 13, 1958. Professionally, he worked as a postman.

MURPHY, WILLIAM (BILL)
Bill became a member on November 11, 1969.

NEWSOME, THOMAS RAY (TOM)
Tom applied for membership on March 11, 2007 and was voted in on May 20, 2007. Unfortunately, Tom had a severe case of Lyme's Disease and was unable to continue. In spite of his condition, he did manage to go to Ohio with the team and was definitely an asset to the show.

"4-Motor Chariot"
Tom Newsome (top left)

"High Pyramid"
Tom Newsome
(2nd tier left)

NOBLE, HARRY

Harry was voted in on May 6, 1970 and was elected President later that year. The team was dwindling in membership and, apparently, they saw a lot of potential in Harry.

NOE, KEITH

Keith joined on March 18, 1995. When he wasn't practicing or doing shows with the team, he worked as a motorcycle funeral escort.

He quit some time in 1996 when he moved to the Midwest to take over his dad's farm.

NOLAN, JERRY

Jerry was a member in the early 1980s.

NORTON, JEREMY

Jeremy applied for membership in 1999. However, because he was a cross country truck driver, it was impossible for him to attend all the practices and perform in the shows. Although he couldn't continue his membership, he was often hired to drive the truck containing the team's motorcycles to some of their long-distance shows. Then, because he was already there, they gave him a uniform and made him part of the show.

Jeremy was lightweight and agile and perfect for the upside down "*Scissors*" or the front fender of the "*Sunflower*."

"Scissors"
Upside Down: Jeremy
Motorman: Mike Betschart
Safety: Sam Watson

"Sunflower"
Front: Jeremy Norton
Motorman: Harry Fisher
Left: Tom Newsome
Right: Sue Hutchings
Safety: Moe Elmore

NUGENT, ROBERT (BOB)

Bob was voted in on March 22, 1984 and retired from the team on July 21, 2002. He rode a beautiful ruby red 1972 Harley and was in the Flag Unit. It wasn't a requirement to have a black and white bike to ride in the Flag Unit and that was ok with Bob.

He was a business owner and operator of a tow truck company.

Bob Nugent

"High Pyramid"
Middle Rear Fender : Bob

O'BRIEN, VERN CHESTER (BUB)

Bub was voted in on November 14, 1969.

ODA, RON

Ron joined the team on July 26, 1992.

OLIVER, NICHOLAS (NICK)

Nick was our next door neighbor and a good friend of Harry's. So, of course, when Harry took over leadership of the team, Nick had to join too.

He was voted in on April 2, 1978 and quit about 1981 when he retired from Rapid Blue Print and moved to Payson, Arizona.

Nick participated in the 20-, 21-, 22- and 23-Men-on-One Motorcycle stunts. In addition to being a good stuntman and drill rider, he was always great fun to have around.

Nick had polio when he was a child and did exercises to stay limber enough to accomplish the stunt work. One exercise he did every morning was a rolling somersault down his hallway. Now that was quite a sight; even more so when he playfully did his rolling somersault at a restaurant and embarrassed his kids!

Created by Tedd Ferrell

"Roman Ride"
Nick Oliver: Top
Harry Fisher: Motorman

"23-Men-On-One Motorcycle"
Nick Oliver on Front Fender

PACKINGHAM, SAM D
Sam was voted into membership on January 5, 1954.

PANTOJA, RUBEN
Ruben first joined the team on August 26, 1979 and quit in 1982.

Ruben Pantoja

Following his retirement as a driver with DeSalvo Trucking, Harry figured Ruben must have some extra time on his hands and might consider joining the team again.

It was during a practice on a Sunday in 2013 that Ruben dropped by to see if anyone might be interested in buying his Motor Corps bike. That was Ruben's purpose for showing up at practice, but it didn't match Harry's. Harry had decided to take advantage of this opportunity. At the time, membership had dwindled down to about five active members, so Harry said, "*Who do you think you're going to sell to? We need members.*" Ruben could see his point.

It just so happened that Mickey Jones had just finished creating his documentary about the team and we were to have a screening event in Simi Valley to show it off. We planned to do a performance outside of the theater first, and then go inside to view the film. We desperately needed members to do the show, so Harry started calling the old timers to see if he could conjure up enough members.

He asked Ruben and, sure enough, Ruben showed up on his old 1972 stunt bike. The team had one practice that morning, were handed uniforms (of some sort) and, together, they put on a great show. Ruben was hooked. He applied for membership (again) and, of course, was voted in once again.

Ruben Pantoja

Ruben was fun to have around as he kept our spirits up. He truly added more "oomph" to the show!

Unfortunately, Ruben passed in 2022.

PARSONS, JAMES H
We believe James became a member some time in 1948. In the late 1990s, we received a very nice letter from his son, Les. Les was a detective with the La Palma Police Department and he happened to see us practicing one day when he was out on patrol. He stopped and we all chatted for a bit.

Below is Les's take on his dad's love of motorcycles and his association with the McLaglen motorcycle team.

"*My father was born in 1921 in Toronto, Canada. He passed away in 1988 in Fullerton, California after a career of wholesale milk delivery. He was a lifelong lover of motorcycles; especially Harley-Davidsons. I think one of the things my dad was most proud of was being a part of the McLaglen motorcycle team. He always spoke very highly of the organization and the people in the organization.*"

PARSONS, JAMES H (Cont'd)

Les showed us a certificate of his dad's membership in the Victor McLaglen Light Horse team. In the 1930s, the Motor Corps members were given membership certificates showing "Victor McLaglen Light Horse" team because the Motor Corps hadn't yet established itself as a separate unit.

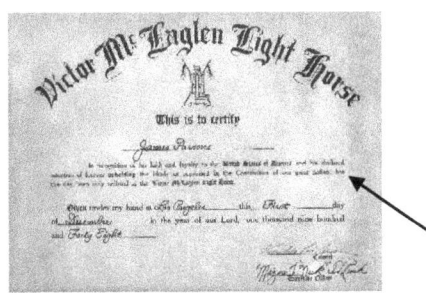

*"In recognition of his faith and loyalty to the **United States of America** and his declared intention of forever upholding the ideals as expressed in the Constitution of our great nation, has this day been duly enlisted in the **Victor McLaglen Light Horse**."*

Signed by Victor McLaglen, Colonel & Major T "Nick" DeRush

**"6-Motor Pyramid"
James Parsons Safetyman**

James Parsons with the Motor Corps

James Parsons – Far Left

PEROTT, JOSEPH WILLIAM (JOE)
Joe was voted in on November 25, 1958 and quit in 1959. Joe rode a 1955 Harley and worked as a finisher.

PERRY, WILLIS L (BILL)
Bill joined the team on November 26, 1963 and quit on April 21, 1964. He rode a 1956 Harley and worked as a machinist.

PETERSON, LARS WALTER
Lars was voted in on March 5, 1957 and quit on July 16, 1957.

PHILLIPS, BILL (WILD BILL)
Wild Bill joined the team in 1937.

Wild Bill

PHILLIPS, EDWIN (EDDIE)
Eddie was a member from about 1937 until the 1940s. He sent the following letter to me in mid-2000. It provides a little more insight into the members of the VMMC.

"Nick DeRush is, or was, the "Father of VMMC." Some way or other, he got Victor McLaglen to foot the bill for uniforms, etc. Each member furnished his own motorcycle which was to be black and white because several members had jobs of conducting funeral groups thru public traffic and used that bike.

How the World Championship came into being was because they challenged the Mexico City Police Motorcycle Team to perform in a tournament and the winner would be determined as World's Champion. The VMMC won and became the World's Champions.

There were three of us Phillips in the Corp: Ray, his cousin and myself. Ray was an airplane pilot and worked for a studio. He would fly the big-shots to "location" and return. He taught me a special stunt which was executed by jumping from the rear stand with the bike in motion to the seat and keep the bike in motion and balanced.

Speaking of stunts: Nick DeRush was the only person I've ever seen that could ride two motorcycles at the same time. He would do this in a large circle with the outmost bike's gas handgrip set at a slightly faster speed than the one on the inner-most bike. With his left foot on the foot rest of the inner and right foot on the outer, he would make a couple of revolutions and have his assistant take control of the inner bike.

We had a 21-man pyramid which consisted of six bikes with drivers plus five standing with the right foot on the bike to his right and left foot on the bike to his left and I was a single on top because I weighed less than anyone else. Hap Ruggles did a fire tunnel because no one else wanted to take over."

PHILLIPS, HERBERT (HUBIE)

Hubie joined the Motor Corps in 1937 and quit in 1943 to join the war effort. This was the case with many of the team members and we are appreciative of their service and their many sacrifices.

In 1939, Hubie was part of the *"21-Men-on-One Motorcycle"* stunt which was performed on a 1936 Harley. According to Hubie's scrapbook, the stunt was accomplished with "no extra equipment other than foot pegs."

Hubie (1943)
U.S. Army Uniform

Hubie (1988)
VMMC Uniform

1939

It was 1988 (age 75) before Hubie returned to the VMMC to support the team. We needed more logo wheel plates for some of the new guys' bikes and Hubie made a bunch of them for the team.

Hubie Hard at Work
Logo Wheel Plates

Finished/Polished
Wheel Plate

"Back Headstand"
Motorman: Hubie
Top: Vern Widdup

Hubie was a very entertaining guy and he had a great sense of humor. His comment regarding the teams' participation in the *"Meet John Doe"* movie, starring Gary Cooper, was *"They gave us a cold chicken box lunch."* The team did very intricate drill maneuvers in this movie and lots of practice to get it perfected. The movie shows quite a bit of footage of the drill.

Lots of smiles and laughter when Hubie was around ...

Hubie & Les Ellis

Harry & Hubie

PHILLIPS, RAYMOND (RAY)

Prior to joining the Motor Corps in the late 1930s, Ray had done everything from hitchhiking to hopping freight trains from Illinois to California; he slept in abandoned cars and washed dishes to survive. On one of his trips to California, he managed to land a job driving actors around the movie studios. It wasn't too long before his passion for motorcycles got him involved with the VMMC and, as you can see from these pictures, he was very talented.

Ray performs his Rope Trick

"Rear Rack One-Legged Ride"
Ray Phillips

In addition to serving as a Corporal for the Motor Corps and proving to be one of the very best stunt riders on the team, Ray was under contract to Universal Pictures as a stuntman. Ray was also a former U.S. Army Officer. Other than that, he was just an ordinary guy. Yep, Ray was a guy who could jump from the rear fender up on to the seat of a moving motorcycle; among other fantastic things! I guess there was actually nothing ordinary about this guy!

In 1982 at age 80 years, Ray lived in the Hollywood Retirement Home in Woodland Hills, California. Some of the Motor Corps members visited to perform a show in his honor. Afterward, he wrote a note thanking the team for a wonderful day. He was thrilled! (See Appendix K for a bio of Ray's life in his own words.)

Ray Phillips stands on the rear rack ..he jumps forward ...   *he lands – and stands on the seat ...*

NO HANDS and NO ONE TO ASSIST!

REESE, JAMES

Although James applied for membership on June 29, 1985, there are no records indicating he became an actual member.

REEVES, WILLIAM ROBERT (BILL)

Bill was voted on to the team on December 13, 1966 and served as Secretary and Vice President before his resignation on November 12, 1968.

According to the meeting minutes of August 8, 1967, Bill's Harley was stolen. Apparently, the notes from the previous meetings and the points list were in his saddlebag, and they were also taken. Points are given to each member for various things; showing up for practice on time, having a clean bike, showing up for a show on time, etc. This seemed the perfect opportunity to reestablish the points system, so they did. After juggling the points around to what they deemed fair, they ended up with Bill Reeves getting the most points and winning the 1st Place trophy at the Annual Banquet for that year.

Bill Reeves	105
Mike Catford	90
Les Georgeson	75
Joe Militello	60
Herb Harker	45
Ronnie Griest	30
George Sterr	15

REID, SAMUEL L

Samuel joined the team on November 26, 1963. On October 27, 1964, he requested a 30-day leave of absence because he was working in Northern California. Two months later (December 8th), he quit the team; probably due to his new work relocation.

Samuel rode a 1957 Harley and worked as a painter.

RESLEY, JEFF

Jeff was voted in on June 1, 1965.

Created by Tedd Farrell

RICKS, ART
Corporal Ricks' name is engraved on the World Championship Trophy.

RISLEY, JEFF
Jeff applied for membership when he was 18 years old. His application was accepted. and he and his 1959 Harley joined the team on June 1, 1965.

ROACH, MRS. HAL (HONORARY MEMBER / 1939-1941)
Marguerite Nichols, a silent film actress who starred in 21 movies from 1915-1918, was married to movie Producer/director Hal Roach for 26 years. She died from pneumonia on March 17, 1941. Mr. Roach died in 1992 at the age of 100. (Wikipedia April 2014)

It was through Producer Roach's association with Victor that she was granted honorary membership and named Lieutenant Colonel of the Victor McLaglen Ladies Troop, later called the Auxiliary. To my knowledge, Ms. Roach never rode or performed with the team

ROBERTS, CHARLES
Charles' name is engraved on the World Championship Trophy.

ROBERTS, JOHN
John joined the Corps on February 28th and quit on November 6, 1961. He rode a 1949 Harley.

ROMERO, JAVIER BAUTISTA
Javier was voted into membership on April 4th and dropped out on July 1, 1993.

RUGGLES, ELMER (HAP)
Hap was one of the original members of the Motor Corps. During his time with the team, he held the titles of Corporal, Sergeant-Major and recording secretary. On the 1936 World Championship Trophy, his name is engraved as Corporal Hap Ruggles. In addition to his key motorman position in many of the stunts, Hap wrote most of the publicity articles which were printed in local newspapers and national motorcycle publications, such as Harley-Davidson's *The Enthusiast Magazine*.

Hap was an active participant with the VMMC until 1949. From 1949 to 1963, he didn't perform with the team; however, he did continue to support the Corps by writing articles. In fact,

(L-R) Crawford & Ruggles

many of the articles and pictures in this book were furnished by his daughter, Deanna (Ruggles) Henderson. Many thanks to her for allowing me to borrow a couple of her huge scrapbooks so I could share Hap's contributions with you. (See Appendix L)

RUIZ, ALBERT II (AL)

Al was voted into membership on September 9, 1978 and quit some time in 1985. He was our Stunt Leader for several years, and was instrumental in training and leading the team. He had a knack for choreographing our performances; he put the right people in the right stunts, in the right order and at the right time. This, of course, led to more spectacular shows.

Al leads "Flying V" formation

"Backward Ride"
Al Ruiz

RUIZ, ALBERT III

Albert (the son of Al Ruiz, II) was just a teenager when he was voted in on August 5, 1979. It was great having another father/son duo on the team.

Al and son Albert

SALSBURY, SHERMAN PAUL (RED)

Red was voted in on May 10, 1955 and served as Vice President in 1956. Professionally, Red worked for the city of Montebello.

SCHAEFER, FREDERICK (FRED)

Fred was voted into membership on July 12th and quit on November 12, 1960.

SCHAEFFER, JOHN G

John joined the Corps on January 10, 1988 and dropped out in early 1992.

SCHAPIRO, STEVE (HONORARY MEMBER 2012)

Steve Schapiro (Schapiro & Leventhal Motorcycle Attorneys) was awarded honorary membership in 2012. Steve was always there when we needed a helping hand, legal counsel, or a bit of financial backing. We were fortunate to have his support and considered him to be a good friend.

Steve Schapiro

SCHIMMEL, ROBERT J (ROB)

Bob was voted on to the team on March 20, 1983 and dropped out on November 24, 1984 (due to his heavy work schedule).

SCHOBERT, CHARLES MURPHY (CHUCK)

Chuck was voted into membership in 1954 and was elected Vice President in 1957. Records are a bit sketchy regarding the remainder of his stint with the Motor Corps. It seems he requested to be placed on inactive status later that year. He must have quit shortly after because he reapplied for membership on November 14, 1960, then dropped off the records again on November 1, 1961.

Left : Chuck Schobert
Right: Theron Willmott

SCHOOLEY, D

Schooley was voted in on June 30, 1970.

SCHEUERS, QUINTON DEAN

Quinton joined on February 2, 1954 and dropped out some time in 1956.

Coincidentally, Elvis Presley released his hit song "Blue Suede Shoes" in 1956. What does this have to do with the Motor Corps? Absolutely nothing! Ha!

SCOTT, TOM & BARBARA (HONORARY MEMBERS 2012)

Tom and Barbara were granted honorary membership in 2012. They had previously owned Anaheim-Fullerton Harley-Davidson and were devoted supporters of the team. They are good friends and even after selling their dealership, they continued to support the team and bring their smiling faces at our events. By the way, they have ridden over 200,000 miles on motorcycles, touring all the western U.S. states many times, three trips to Europe from Germany south through Yugoslavia down into Greece, crossed over to Italy on a freighter, then rode north through Switzerland, Austria, back to Frankfurt, then back home. Of course, they also rode many escorted rides with Willie G. and Nancy Davidson, compliments of the Victor McLaglen Motor Corps.
(See Appendix M)

Tom and Barbara Scott

SENTER, JOHN M

John joined the team on April 6, 1954 and quit on April 6, 1959. John was a retired Los Angeles police officer.

SESSLER, LEE GRANULLE

Lee was riding his 1953 Harley when he was voted in on November 18, 1958.

SEVILLA, GUILLERMO, SR

Guillermo joined the team on May 21, 1989, but found it necessary to quit a couple of years later because of work constraints. Prior to his retirement from the Tijuana, Mexico Police Department where he also participated with the Suicide Squadron Motorcycle Stunt Team, he joined the Santa Monica, California Police Department. It took his retirement from this second career before he was able to reapply for membership with the VMMC in 2013. He never truly left the team, however, as three of his sons also became members. It is definitely a "family affair."

Guillermo.

Guillermo is a good, strong motorman and he and his family are definite assets to the team.

SEVILLA, GUILLERMO, JR. (JUNIOR) and MICHAEL

As teenagers, Junior and Michael, first joined the team with their father on May 21, 1989. It seems they followed their dad's lead. Then they dropped out and a few years later, in 2013, they reapplied for membership.

SEVILLA, RENE

Rene joined the team along with his brothers and Father and became the Assistant Stunt Leader. It's great to have an entire family working together.

As a stuntman, Rene is superb. He always has a smile and seems to love entertaining the crowd. He has developed a couple of new stunts and does them with a flourish.

It's a "Sevilla Family Affair"
Rene, Michael, & Guillermo

SHANAHAN, PATRICK (PAT)

Pat applied for membership on August 21, 1984, and was accepted on September 21st following his retirement as a Texaco truck driver. He quit the team in 1999 and moved to Billings, Montana but remained committed to the team. When Harry was laid up recovering from a serious motorcycle accident, Pat was called. Harry needed him to drive the truck for the next three months, transporting motorcycles across country for the International Motorcycle Shows. He continues to keep in touch with his teammates and is always available to help, however and whenever he is able.

SHERMAN, GARY

Gary was voted in on November 17, 1953. Gary worked for the U.S. Air Force Weather Station in Long Beach, California.

SMITH, BILL

Bill joined on June 7, 1955 and quit on November 6, 1957. It appears Bill wanted to be a member of the Corps as records show him joining and quitting … and joining again. He was voted in on February 24, 1961; he quit on October 3, 1961; he joined again in 1995; unfortunately, there is no further information after 1995.

Created by Tedd Farrell

Note: To explain this cartoon for the non-Motor Corps folks, "break it down" is what the motorman yells when he wants all the riders to return to their original start-off position; i.e., sitting on the bike, standing on the bike, hugging close to the center of gravity on the bike, etc. They "break it down" when the stunt is completed, when something goes wrong or when there is a need to abort.

SMITH, ELLIS (SMITTY)

Like many men in the 1930-40s, Smitty's life was impacted by World War II. His enlistment in the U.S. Navy in 1938 stationed him in Hawaii where he suffered a wound to his right leg on December 7th at Pearl Harbor. After receiving an Honorable Discharge, Smitty returned stateside to motorcycling and truck driving.

From 1943-1944, he participated in numerous dare devil stunt and thrill shows. This prompted him to join the Victor McLaglen Motor Corps and he was voted in on May 26, 1970. During his time with the Corps, Smitty attained the ranks of Corporal, Sergeant, Staff Sergeant and, finally, Lieutenant. In addition to being a terrific motorman and team supporter, Smitty stayed on to help the team reorganize in 1978. He retired a few years later.

"P-38"
Motorman Smitty

"2-Motor Pushup"
Motormen: Lyle Carmody, Smitty,
Joe Militello
Motormen

1978 - Smitty & Wife, Margaret

"Horse"
Tylor Hicks: Top
Smitty: Motorman

SNOW, BOB J (BOBBY)

Bobby was voted in on October 16, 1962 and quit on December 10, 1962. This team isn't for everybody. It's good to find that out early.

SNOW, DONALD HOWARD (DON)

It all began in 1965 when Don attended the Death Valley Run where the VMMC was performing. Don temporarily left the show to grab a bite to eat. He was patiently waiting in the chow line when Corporal Harry Fisher (about 20 years old at the time) decided to take cuts. After a few meaningful words, the two got better acquainted and Harry invited Don to join the team. Don showed up for practice, liked it and completed an application. He was voted in by the membership on August 24, 1965.

The most difficult part of joining the Corps was when he had to cover up the gorgeous red paint job on his 1965 Harley Electra Glide with the standard black and white pattern (a requirement for all team members). He begrudgingly did it.

In 1966, Don brought a special guest to his practice. His sister, Ruth, was visiting and he wanted to show off the team. But that wasn't all he wanted; Don also wanted to introduce Ruth to Harry.

The two hit it off pretty good and the following week, Harry invited Ruth to the Hollywood Christmas Parade. The Victor McLaglen Motor Corps opened the parade and, of course, Ruth was pretty impressed.

Harry had it all figured out. After picking her up in his 1964 Harley, he escorted her to the top step of the Hollywood Masonic Lodge; a strategic spot for watching the parade. After the parade was over, Harry circled around, picked up Ruth and took her for a cup of coffee. You could say he swept her off her feet.

A few years later, Harry and Ruth were married and they remained together for 43 years until Harry's death. They have one son, Marty, who was also an instrumental member of the Motor Corps, and a grandson, Joshua. Only time will tell whether Joshua will follow the motorcycling path of his father and grandfather.

"Frame Ride"
Don Snow

Don (right) receives Membership Certificate from Colonel Harker - 1965

Harry & Ruth Brought Together by Big Brother, Don

SOTO, RIGOBERTO (RIGO)

When Rigo joined the team in 2011, he knew nothing about stunt riding … but, then, neither did many of Motor Corps recruits. It was definitely Just-In-Time (JIT) / On-The-Job (OTJ) training. It wasn't long before Rigo learned how to do the drill without running into anyone. In fact, he progressed to become a motorman for many of the stunts.

Rigo Soto

"Horse"
Rigo & Mark

SPOON, CHARLES WILSON (CHUCK)

Chuck was first voted into membership on August 6, 1963, and dropped out July 21, 1965. He returned again on December 13th, but dropped out a year later.

Mr. and Mrs. Chuck Spoon
1965 Motor Corps Awards Banquet

STACKEM, CHESTER (GERALD)

Gerald was voted into membership on January 15, 1957. He was employed by the City of Montebello.

STAFFORD, LEO R

Leo joined the Corps on September 22, 1970.

STAGNER, WALT

Walt was voted in on July 15, 1969 and quit on May 18, 1970. In 1970, he served as Sergeant at Arms and Motor Corps SCMA representative in 1970.

STAPERT, JOHN R

John was voted into membership in 1957. He worked at Urich Motor Company in Whittier, California.

STARKEY, CHESTER GERALD (JACK)

Jack was voted in on January 15th and quit on September 10, 1957.

STERR, GEORGE R (BILL)

Bill joined the membership on June 20, 1967. He served as Club Secretary in 1969 and he quit on August 26th. He rode a 1962 Harley and worked as a draftsman.

STEWART, JOEL

Joel joined the team in 1935 and his name is engraved on the World Championship Trophy.

In the early 1930s, Joel mastered the front position of the "Ladder Headstand." He would stand on the front crash bars, brace himself against the handebars and use his shoulders to support the ladder while a team member was wiggling around upside down. You need to note that there were NO hands and NO helmets! This was a four-man stunt that involved a motorman, a man in front and one in the rear holding the ladder and, of course, the upside-down guy on the ladder.

"Stretcher Handstand"
Front Ladder Man: Joel Stewart
Rear Ladder Man: Hap Ruggles
Up Ladder Man: Jimmy Crawford
Motorman: Nick DeRush

"Swan"
Rear: Joel Stewart
Up: Jimmy Crawford
Motorman: Hap Ruggles

STILTZ, BUD

Bud joined the Corps on October 4, 1960. He rode a 1960 Harley and worked as a welder.

STILTS, TOM

Tom was voted in on September 27, 1960 and quit on July 18, 1961.

STINT, O B (OB)

OB joined the VMMC on November 3, 1953.

STOCKWELL, RONALD C (RONNIE)

Ronnie was riding a 1956 Harley when he joined the team on May 23, 1961; he quit on September 9, 1962.

STROUD, JACK

Jack was in the Motor Corps some time in the 1940s. I was unable to find further information on Jack, however, below are a couple of pictures.

Jack Stroud

Jack and his sister

STUTTS, JOHN PATTERSON (PAT)

Pat joined the team in 1941. His son told me Pat rode his 1930 Harley from Los Angeles, California to Charlotte, North Carolina in the 40s. That was before the comforts of the new Harleys nowadays. Quite a feat.

Unfortunately, years later, he had a tragic highway wreck on his Harley while in route to escort a funeral and spent long months recuperating. In fact, he endured seven major operations on his mangled leg.

Pat Stutts

Pat Stutts and his stunt bike

SUSSLER, LEE G

Lee was voted in on November 18, 1958.

SUTCLIFFE, W M (LEE)

Although Dr. Sutcliffe was not a riding member, he served as Activity Director and Master of Ceremonies in 1936.

SWAN, BILL

Bill was a member of the team in 1936 and performed the fire-tunnel stunt. This event took place in the Los Angeles Coliseum prior to their competition against the Mexico City's "Squadron of Death" motorcycle riders.

SWAN, BILL (Cont'd)

Bill's name is engraved on the World Championship Trophy.

"Fire-Tunnel Stunt"
Bill Swan competes with "Squadron of Death"

A THRILL FOR 40,000 persons was the excursion through leaping flames taken by Bill Swan, motorcycle expert from Victor McLaglen's Light Horse Troop, yesterday at the Coliseum. A large tent, made of burlap, was saturated with gasoline and set on fire.

> *Swan went through the blaze at 65 miles an hour, with only ordinary cyclist's equipment. Speed protected the rider, his clothing and motorcycle from burns. The stunt was a feature of a show staged by the Police Department.*
>
> Daily News Photo.

Note: Getting the rider ready for the Fire-Wall or tunnel requires taping the sleeves and pants cuffs so no fire can enter them, putting a scarf or mask over the face and neck, wearing good quality goggles, a full-face helmet, good leather gloves and boots, and either a fire-proof jumpsuit or one made of heavy cotton. Any polyester or nylon in the fabric will cause it to melt onto the rider's skin. Obviously, not a desirable experience!

SWANSON, JAMES STANLEY I (JIM)

Jim Swanson joined the team in 1965 when he was about 38 years old. He bought a 1965 light blue, electric-start Harley. This bike was the third electric-start Harley sold in California. With Johhny Kazian's help, they repainted the bike to the required black and white colors of the Motor Corps.

At the time, Jim's son, Butch, was only 10 years old. He thought it was the greatest thing in the world to clean and polish his dad's bike, so he could perform with the Motor Corps. The kid's goal was to make his dad's Harley look shinier than any other bike on the team. I don't know if he succeeded, but I do know that years later, James Swanson II (Butch) joined the Corps to follow in his Dad's footsteps.

Among many other stunts, both father and son mastered the spectacular *"Spread Eagle"* stunt (see next page for photo).

Jim and his new 1965 Harley

Prepping for Show Time

"Rear Rack Ride"
Residential street in Lakewood, California
No cops in sight!

SWANSON, JAMES S JR (BUTCH)

Butch (son of James Sr.) was voted into membership on December 2, 2007. He joined the team after attending a practice session in La Palma, California. He was a quick learner with drill maneuvers and Harry began priming him for stunts.

"Inside Basket"
Butch (left)

"Slow Circle"
Butch (front axle)

"Spread Eagle"
Butch (middle)

TANURAHARJO, BENNY

Benny applied for membership in 2011, participated in a couple of shows and then dropped out.

TATRO, WILFRED J

Wilfred was voted in on March 9, 1954.

TAYLOR, EMMET CLIFFORD (CLIFF)

Cliff was voted in on September 1, 1959 and quit on January 30, 1976. He rode a 1956 Harley.

TEMPLET, GEORGE W (BILL)

Bill was voted in on April 27th and quit the same year on July 24, 1965. He worked for the U.S. Navy and rode a 1958 Harley.

THOMAS, ALVIN

Alvin's name is engraved on the World Championship Trophy.

THOMPSON, GERALD L (JERRY)

Jerry was voted in on September 17, 1978. He worked as a delivery truck driver (33 years) for the Los Angeles Times. Jerry also rode with the old AMA Road Riders group from 1967-1972.

Jerry quit in 1985 when he sold his Harley to buy a boat.

TURNBULL, WILLIAM

William was introduced to the Corps by team member, Joe Militello. He weighed about 130 lbs, so was the perfect candidate for top man on the pyramid. He performed at the Death Valley Motorcycle Run.

UNDERWOOD, JIM

Jim joined the Motor Corps in 1941. He was employed at Northrop where he worked on the P-61 Black Widow aircraft.

VASQUEZ, THOMAS WAYNE (TOM)

Tom was voted in June 7, 1966. He worked as an electrician and rode a 1960 Harley.

VIRGIN, GLENN ORIS

Glenn was voted in August 23, 1981 and quit in1982. He was also President of the State Line Riders Motorcycle Club in Lompoc, California.

WADDELL, LOUIE MORTON IV

Louie received his membership on May 15, 1981 and quit in 1982. He worked at the former Chubbuck's Harley-Davidson in Pasadena, California.

WALES, ARTHUR ALLEN (ART)

The Motor Corps accepted Art as a team member on June 10, 1984. He left in 1990 to attend the police academy and eventually joined the San Bernardino, California Sheriff's Department.

"Spread Eagle"
Art (horizontal/middle)
Motormen Harry (left) and Marty (right)

Vintage Days 2007
Lexington, Ohio

WALKER, JOHN (JOHNNY)

Johnny was a former professional skateboarder along with Ray Kult. They both quit skateboarding and joined the team in 1992. Neither one of them had a motorcycle, however, they were terrific at climbing to the top of the Pyramid, doing headstands and performing various other stunts.

WARREN, DONALD (DON)

Don was voted in three different times (July 1, 1975, October 8, 1978 and June 28, 1992). As a member of the team, he rode a side car which displayed the flag and acted as the lead-in participant for parades and shows. As a profession, Don was a motorcycle mechanic.

Don had Berger's Disease, which eventually resulted in the amputation of his leg. Even with a prosthesis, Don was able to ride a motorcycle. In fact, he and others on the team were hired by a movie company to film a commercial for Budweiser Beer. They traveled to Utah, put on Shriner-like costumes (with cute, little pointy-toed shoes with bells on them) and rode a drill formation for the commercial. They all had a great time and made a bit of money too.

Don rides sidecar w/Ruth Fisher (announcer)

Don & the Crew Budweiser Beer Commercial

WATCHBORG, MARSHAL

Marshal was voted in on January 26, 1954.

WATKINS, DENNIS WILBERT

Dennis' request for membership was accepted on May 31, 1966. He rode a 1953 Harley and worked as a truck driver. Records show he rode in the Montebello and Canoga Park parades.

WATSON, RAY OTTO

Ray was voted in on January 28, 1958 and February 6, 1962, and resigned on July 20, 1965. Ray was 18 when he first joined, and participated with his brother, Sam Jr., and dad, Sam Sr.

Rumor has it Ray and Harry Fisher would coordinate their arrival time to practice, race into the parking lot together, slide sideways, and come to a screeching halt. Being young and a little crazy, they thought it was great fun. Needless to say, Colonel Herb Harker was not pleased with their shenanigans!

Ray Watson 23 years old

WATSON, SAM JR (SAM)

Sam first applied for membership on April 16, 1963 (age 19). His brother, Ray, had been voted in the prior year, and his dad, Sam Sr., had been a member for eight years.

He stayed active for a couple of years, but left the team on April 21, 1965 when he was drafted into the U.S. Army. He served a couple of years as an electrician and prisoner escort from his base in Ft. Riley, Kansas to Oakland Army Base in California. One thing led to another and he got married, started a family and said goodbye to the Corps.

Sam Watson
1967 FLH

His absence, however, was short lived when he and his wife, Claudia, attended the 1995 Annual Motor Corps in Laughlin, Nevada. They watched a couple of shows in front of the casino and Claudia asked him, "*Do you think you'd like to join up again?*" Well, I guess that was all it took, because on July 17, 1995, Sam applied for membership (again) and was voted in on October 29, 1995.

"Fan"
Sam: Safety Man (middle)

"Bridge"
Sam: Safety Man (front crash bar)

"Spread Eagle"
Sam: Motorman (left)

WATSON, SAM JR (SAM) (Cont'd)

Sam bought an old 1956 Ford pickup and completely restored it to add a few improvements like air condition and a souped-up engine. He even included a 4.6 police interceptor motor that had him clocked at going 112 mph!

Sam used the pickup truck (customized license plate HD Haler) to pull the trailer with his stunt bike onboard. He definitely got lots of attention.

Sam's Customized 1956 Ford

WATSON, SAM SR (SAM)

Sam was voted into the club on October 4, 1955 and was elected Secretary from 1957-58. He enjoyed performing all the stunts and loved riding his Harley.

Sam Watson Sr.

It was definitely a *Family Affair* as "The Watson Boys" (father and two sons) performed with the Victor McLaglen Motor Corps.

Father & sons, all members of the corps, perfected this formation, called the P-38 because of its resemblance to the World War II fighter plane of the same designation.

"The Watson Boys"

WEAVER, RICHARD DELL
Richard was voted in on September 9, 1975 and resigned a year later.

WEISBERG, SAM
Sam was voted in on October 21, 1962 and rode a 1955 Harley. Because his work took him out of the country for several months at a time, Sam quit on August 8, 1963.

WELCH, DANIEL LEROY (DAN)
Dan was voted in on September 21, 1994. He bought the team's stunt bike from Dick Gerry and intended to keep it in the Corps. This did not happen, however, as he left in about 2003.

Dan was the first guy in the Motor Corps to ace the "Scissors," which is a handstand on the handlebars. He was followed by Jeremy Norton in the 1990s and, finally, Rene Sevilla in 2013.

Dan Welch

"Pyramid"
Dan (top)
Motorcycle Lift Ad - 1994

"Scissors"
Dan (upside down)

WELCH, PAIGE
Paige was only 15 years old when he joined the team. He was voted in on August 10, 2003, but left shortly thereafter. His father, Dan Welch, was also a member of the Motor Corps.

WELDEN, JAMES (JIM)
Jim joined on September 9, 1961. During his time with the Motor Corps, Jim worked in a machine shop and rode a 1959 Harley.

He quit on September 11, 1962 because his bike was stolen. He was reinstated on November 5, 1962, but left less than a year later on March 21, 1963.

WEST, WILLIAM H (BILL)
Bill was initially voted in as a non-riding member on September 8, 1953. He joined again on April 22, 1958.

WHITE, HARVEY L

Even though Harvey rode a 1974 HONDA, he was somehow voted in on October 22, 1974. Hmmmm ... a HONDA? Don't know how he got in, but he proved himself with his promotion to Corporal in 1976.

Harvey was employed at Douglas Aircraft Company as an instrument repair and calibration technician in the Metrology Lab.

WHITESELL, ERNEST LEROY (ERNIE)

Ernie rode a 1977 Harley and was voted into membership on November 15, 1981.

The following year, Ernie wrote a letter to the officers suggesting how he might assist with the team's administrative duties. In the letter, he stated, "*I don't have the riding ability to be Commander, but I can type, make phone calls, help in scheduling, make arrangements, and I am capable of learning anything that someone else is capable of teaching me.... We are carrying on a tradition. I have heard bits and pieces of the history of the Victor McLaglen Motor Corps. I don't think I have heard it all, but I do know that participation has been up and down to the point where the Corps has been reduced to a riding club at times and has been inactive for a while. I would like to be instrumental in keeping the Corps alive and performing!*"

Time and time again, the McLaglen Motor Corps has demonstrated this kind of dedication and conviction from its members. This support is what has helped to keep the team alive all these years.

WIDDUP, VERN

Vern joined the team in 1936. In 2011, Vern's stepson, Jack Barber, sent a note to the Motor Corps website describing some of Vern's experiences with the Victor McLaglen Motor Corps.

"Nice to see the Corps is still alive.

My stepdad, Vern Widdup, was an original member with Nick DeRush in the early years. He was a tool and die instructor at Santa Monica Technical School. He designed and made the logo wheel mounted disc which was installed on every motor.

Logo Wheel

I remember, in the '40s, the Corps worked the Rose Parade. Dad would often take me for a ride and also do stunts with me sitting on the back of his bike."

Vern & his lovely Wife

WIDDUP, VERN (Cont'd)

"Vern was born in Iowa in 1900 and died in Los Angeles in 1990. During his early years in Iowa, he rode saddle broncs and brahma bulls in rodeos. Except for his arthritis, caused by falls from horses and bulls and his motorcycle, he was quite healthy."

"Rear Rack Ride" *Vern (upside down)* *Vern manhandling his bike*
Vern Widdup *Hubie Phillips (bike)*

WIDODO, AGUS (DODO)

Dodo joined the team in 2011. While practicing one of his stunts, something went wrong and Dodo broke his ankle. Unfortunately, he had to spend a couple of months on the sidelines.

WILLAMAN, DAN

Dan applied for membership on April 21, 1992 and was accepted shortly thereafter. He moved to Nebraska and had to quit the team.

WILLERS, MARIA M

Maria and her bright, red 1972 Harley Shovelhead were accepted into the Corps on July 30, 2000. Of course, the first order of business was to repaint her bike to meet the regulation black and white color scheme. She was reluctant to do it, but agreed.

In addition to being a skilled biker, Maria was the first woman to become a full-fledged drill-riding member of the team.

Maria Willers

Maria's introduction to the Victor McLaglen Motor Corps occurred when she attended a show at the Yuma Prison Run in Arizona. She was introduced to Harry (the leader of the team), talked a bit, watched the show, rode home, then showed up at practice the following week to apply for membership. She practiced every day until

WILLERS, MARIA M (Cont'd)

she could master riding slow, slipping the clutch and making those ultra-sharp turns required for drill riding. She got very good with these skills but also was very good with the crowds, interacting with the fans, shaking hands, answering questions, signing autographs, and always wearing a huge smile.

Maria wrote several articles for motorcycle enthusiasts. One of the articles, *"The Maria Willers' Story – Everything you have ever wanted to know about joining a motorcycle stunt and drill team, but were afraid to try,"* was published in *ThunderPress.* (See Appendix N)

Maria's move to Caliente, Nevada in 2003 resulted in her resignation.

Maria rides the drill

Maria & one of her new fans

"Speedo"
Maria (left)
Mark Frymoyer (right)

WILLIAMSON, WILLIAM (BILL)

Bill's membership was brief. He was voted in on February 25, 1964 and resigned on July 21, 1964. Bill rode a 1956 Harley and worked as a furniture salesman.

WILMOTT, THERON

Theron was voted into membership on December 6, 1955 and quit in 1957 to join the U.S. Armed Forces. He returned to the Motor Corps after he was discharged from the military, but quit again on June 4, 1962. Theron served as the VMMC Secretary in 1960 and President in 1961.

In 2002, the team received a letter from Theron's son, Steve Wilmott, who at that time, was Vice President of the Arkansas State Bank. Steve stated, *"Dad says to tell you all "Hi" and hope you are doing well. He sold his poultry farm about a year ago and bought a house and 20 acres. They are enjoying not having to worry about the farm anymore."*

WOLFE, KYLE J

He was voted into membership on August 19, 1958. Kyle rode a 1955 Harley and was employed as a truck driver.

WOOD, RICHARD KENT (RICH)

Rich was voted in on October 21, 1993. He and Ray Mehlbaum saw the team perform and thought, "*Why not?*," so they both joined. They were real assets to the shows. They worked the crowds for responses, perfected their riding skills and became true "team" members.

Rich was a strong Safetyman in many of the stunts, as well as hanging out on the "P-38" or sitting on the driver's shoulders while performing the "Totem Pole." TRUST is an important part of the stunts and the guys could always depend on Rich.

Rich (left) riding drill with Tylor Hicks

"Half P-38"
Rich "hanging out"
with Harry Fisher

"Totem Pole"
International Motorcycle Show
New York City
Rich: Middle
Mike: Motorman
Mickey: Top

Note: The P-38 stunt was named after the WWII U.S. fighter plane.

WOODARD, ROBERT E (WOODY)

Woody was voted into membership on April 29, 1984.

He was a Chief Boiler Technician in the U.S. Navy supervising the boiler rooms which steam to the main engines of the ship. He retired from the Navy on February 29, 1988, and his move to Sacramento in 1989 led to his resignation from the Motor Corps.

Woody's performance as Stuntman and Motorman were indeed assets to the team.

Woody sporting his Motor Corps uniform in the show

WRIGHT, JOHN W

John was voted in on November 18, 1986. In addition to his VMMC membership, John served as a funeral escort motorcycle rider.

WYRICK, WILLIAM EUGENE (BILL)

Bill was accepted into the Corps on April 21, 1976. He rode a 1968 Harley and worked as a planner at Douglas Aircraft Company in Long Beach, California.

YAWN, WADE

Wade was voted in on April 2, 1957. Wade was employed at the Chrysler Corporation.

ZELENAK, RICHARD J (DICK)

Dick's relationship with the Corps spanned several years. He was first voted in on August 6, 1963, but requested a "leave of absence" on October 20, 1964 because he needed to have his motorcycle engine overhauled.

He took to the road in March of 1965 and joined the circus. Eventually he returned to the Corps and was voted in on December 13, 1965. Dick rode both a 1949 and a 1959 Harley.

Created by Tedd Farrell

Appendix A

Louis Michael (Mike) Betschart

During Mike's career in the United States, he worked for a couple of employers; however, exclusively he was a Mercedes-Benz mechanic and very good at the task. He decided to open his own shop in 1990 and ran it successfully for the next 17 years. In 2007, after 'wrenching' for 41 years, Mike decided that was enough and sold the business to try something new.

In 2010, I asked Mike to send me a story about his life including his time in Switzerland and the United States, his working career, his experiences with the Motor Corps, and his family. I found it very interesting. It reminded me that we often think we know someone when we really don't have a clue.

"I was born in Lynwood, California on July 17, 1950 to Swiss parents. We lived in Norwalk, California and attended St. John of God Catholic School through 8th grade."

"The family moved to Switzerland, where I finished my schooling and lived in Schwyz in the central part of Switzerland. One day, when I was walking down from a nearby mountain, I came across a farmer. After chatting with him for a while, I found out that he owned a Lambretta that he didn't want anymore. (Lambretta is a line of motor scooters originally manufactured in Milan, Italy by Innocenti.) Naturally, being a kid, I showed interest and he gave the 125cc scooter to me. Happily, I rode it down the mountain, coasting all the way home (the motor wasn't running) and immediately started to tinker with it. This was the start of my lifelong love of motorcycles."

"I started a four-year apprenticeship in Brunnen at the Lake of Lucern as an auto mechanic at 16 years old, then graduated and started work. When I started my apprenticeship, I graduated to a moped, which didn't need a driver's license to operate. (Swiss law didn't allow anyone to have a driver's license until the age of 18.) This moped went only 18 mph which was waaayyyy too slow for me. I souped up the engine and got it to run at 45 mph. Next, I bought a Prior 50cc scooter (Sachs engine) with a 5-speed transmission followed by a 1950 Sunbeam 500cc, 2-cylinders in-line, which came stock with 16" wheels and was a Harley look-alike. I paid 50 francs for it (approximately $15 USD) and, again, it was not running. I stripped the bike down, painted it, and finally had it running. After about two months of riding, the exhaust flex pipe broke, causing the engine to backfire, and burned up the new paint. I rode this bike for about a quarter of a mile while it was aflame and arrived at my workplace to use the fire extinguisher. Unfortunately, the extinguisher was faulty and the bike burned to a crisp."

"Since they did not play football in Europe, I joined the town soccer team. I also joined a wrestling team (youth group) where I was undefeated but had to quit because I had too much homework to do. My future was more important to me. Of course, my coach was not very happy because he was looking to go to the nationals with me. I also belonged to the Swiss Youth Mountaineers, a mountain climbing group. In those days, rappelling from an overhanging cliff down a 1000-foot drop did not bother me. Today, just looking down from a second story sends a chill up my spine -- go figure."

"I was also a very active spelunker, and enjoyed riding and racing a skibob during wintertime (a low-slung frame which looks similar to a bicycle on skis). I raced for many years, always coming in second behind my friend, who was just a hair faster. In 1967, I was called to join a rescue mission in Switzerland which lasted for four days. The cave is called Hell's Hole and it still has not been totally mapped. Hell's Hole is a vast array of caverns and arms extending over a hundred miles in every direction like a spider web. Initially, I was only scheduled to carry backpacks, but I ended up helping carry the stretcher with a hurt spelunker for eight hours through the deepest, most dangerous part of the cave. When the weather changes, this part of the cavern fills up with water in three minutes, but takes six hours to traverse."

"In 1972, I bought my next bike which was a 1965 650cc Triumph Bonneville. This was from a corporal whom I had met in boot camp. I had been a mechanic in the Swiss Army where I repaired and drove motorcycles, jeeps, big trucks and other vehicles, and he thought I needed this bike. The Triumph was great fun and handled really well through the narrow twisting roads, but had electrical problems (Lucas)."

"After buying the Triumph in Switzerland, I rode through town (a small tourist town on Lake Lucerne) doing various stunts; for example: floorboard ride (but no floorboards - just foot pegs), seat ride, side saddle ride, laying on seat, feet crossed over handlebars, and kneeling on the seat, riding hands-off. I had to stop this kind of nonsense because I got caught by the local police, who let me off with just a warning. (You see, I was the mechanic who fixed their police boat!)"

"In 1973, I married Heidy in St. Gallen, Switzerland and moved to St. Gallen (north eastern part of Switzerland). 1973 was also a big year for me because it was the same year I became a shop manager and started supervising a crew of 23 mechanics."

"In November 1976, I had my training and some experience under my belt and decided to return to the USA to find a job and a place to live. I succeeded with this plan and a year later, my wife, Heidy, and the kids immigrated to the USA and joined me. Immigration rules were strict even then and the process seemed to take forever."

"My next motorcycle (after returning to California) was a 1971 750cc Norton Commando. I sold this one a few years before I joined the Motor Corps, but managed to do a lot of successful street racing for beers with this bike."

"Before joining the Motor Corps, the family and I were active off-roaders on bikes and a homebuilt sand-rail. Weekends were spent on a dry lake or in Glamis, California on the sand dunes. When hunting season started, I went bird hunting with some friends while my wife hoped I wouldn't hit anything so she wouldn't have to cook it (doves, pheasants and ducks)."

"Why did I joined the Motor Corps? For a couple years, starting in 1986, a tow-truck driver, Bob Nugent, who joined the Motor Corps in 1984, would come by my shop every so often and try to talk me into coming down to watch the Victor McLaglen Motor Corps practice and join the team. He would tease me that they would teach me how to really ride a motorcycle. Of course, my response was, 'Ha, ha.' After all, I knew all about riding and didn't need these guys to teach me anything. Finally, I gave in and watched them practice at the Downey Elks Lodge in Downey, California. After watching the second practice, I told myself, 'I can do this' ... and then I was hooked. I bought my first Harley 1975 FLH (never rode one before) from Bob Nugent, which was formerly Jerry Thompson's bike, another former member."

Practicing Drill   **Mike after a Sunday Practice**

"When I first joined the Motor Corps, Bob would always tease me about trailering the bike. 'You need to get some road experience.' His teasing stopped when we did a poker run up Highway 2 in the Angeles Mountains. I took off, thoroughly enjoying the twists and turns on the mountain. When we finally regrouped, the only comment from Bob was, 'Boy, you get Mike up in these mountains and he thinks he's in the Alps!' Needless to say, he never teased me again!"

"In 1988, when I joined the Motor Corps, I bought a 1975 Harley FLH and it became my Motor Corps stunt and drill bike. I also purchased a 1985 Yamaha Venture Royal for just cruising through the countryside and 1935 Harley VLD just for historical reasons; but the FLH is the one I spent the bulk of my time riding in the Motor Corps shows. We practiced almost every Sunday and, in between practices, performed a bunch of shows on this bike and it just hung right in there."

"My first parade was the Lynwood Christmas Parade and my first infield show was Love Ride IV. But, my first stunt ever was when I was three years old. I had a rooster who sat on my left shoulder while I was riding my tricycle up and down the block. That show often stopped traffic. Now I'm doing stunts with 160-pound men and women standing on both shoulders and more."

"In 1991, I joined Masonry, became Master in 1997, coached for three years and then became Inspector for seven years, overseeing three Masonic Lodges."

"Heidy and I raised three children. My daughter, Priska, is married to Shawn, and is a homemaker and mother of Jason, Alex and Brian. (Priska was the first female to actually do stunts in our Motor Corps shows, but she never actually became a member and didn't ride a motorcycle in the drill. I was very proud to see her participate, along with Ruben Pantoja's daughter, Alex. This was before Maria Willers actually joined, and rode in the drill and stunts.) My oldest son, Steven, is a B-1 bomber pilot and unmanned predator pilot in the United States Air Force. My youngest son, Allan, is married to Sabine. Allan is a former Motor Corps Member and joined when he was a teenager. He is now a Computer Programming Engineer in Illinois and has a son, Oz."

"Some 30+ years later, Heidy and I are still happily married and live in Illinois near our youngest son, Allen."

Mike Betschart

Mike in show uniform on his 1975 stunt bike

Unfortunately, Mike passed away in 2011 after his retirement and move to Illinois. He was definitely missed.

Appendix B

Malcolm Bruce Chubbuck

Bruce Chubbuck's life was always ALL about motorcycles. In a June 1998 article of *Iron Works* magazine entitled, "*Bruce Chubbuck: A Harley Life,*" Margie Stegal writes, "*Until he was two, Bruce traveled around with his mother in the sidecar outfit, which was bolted to a Harley JD. His first bike was a 125cc two stroke.*" It was definitely a family affair.

Before Bruce's father, Chubby, entered into the Harley-Davidson business in California, he owned a business in Roxbury, Massachusetts.

In 1927, Chubby relocated to California. He bought out P.A. Bigsby's half share in the Pasadena Harley-Davidson dealership and became partners with the other owner, Bill Graves. When the partnership split in 1951, Bruce worked full-time for his father at Chubbuck Harley-Davidson in Pasadena, California. Chubby passed in 1976, and Bruce took over ownership and the running of the business until December 31, 1983, when he closed the doors. He said he didn't go broke. He just didn't want to do it anymore.

In April 1984, Bruce found himself at the Harley-Davidson Motor Company's main headquarters in Milwaukee where he signed on to be the manager of the new Harley-Davidson West Coast Fleet Test Center. He served in this capacity until the age of 69 when he retired from Harley on February 1, 2000.

This 1936 "61 OHV" as it was found in Pasadena October 12 1979. It had been parked since 1947. Pictured on right is Rolland Frehn owner for 41 years on bike after 45 minutes of steam cleaning plus 3 more hours & 2 quarts of gunk. Small picture shows Rolland on the "61" at Puddingstone Dam over looking San Dimas October 12, 1938. Below as it appeared on a poster July 1986 – 50 years old.

One of Bruce's Restoration Projects
1936 Harley

Hot Dog Bikes magazine, "Bruce Chubbuck" (Kendall, K.R., June 2000)

Bruce Chubbuck

MORE THAN 50 YEARS IN MOTORCYCLING

TEXT BY K. RANDALL BALL
PHOTOS COURTESY OF BRUCE CHUBBUCK

Bruce Chubbuck remembers his father as a young man, wrapping him in a blanket and handing him to his mother, who was sitting in a JD sidecar...during the winter. He's never been the same. From that day forward, he's been in motorcycling—through his father's dealership, as an owner, and finally, for the last 16 years, as the sole employee, manager, and executive of Harley-Davidson's growing fleet center in California. In 1977 at a new-model announcement meeting for dealers in Las Vegas, Bruce was caught completely off guard when the Factory awarded him with a 50-year award for his service to motorcycling and to Harley-Davidson.

Bruce is also an avid motorcycle racing fan and a long-standing 21-year member of the Victor McLaglen stunt and drill team. Below he reflects on the past, the decades of ups and downs with the motorcycle industry, and his life's blood—the Harley-Davidson factory.

HRB: *Give us a brief overview of your history in motorcycling.*

Bruce: My dad, "Chubby," was a Harley-Davidson dealer when I was born. Then in high school I started working at the dealership, which I got class credits for. My dad's dealership, Graves and Chubbuck Harley-Davidson in Pasadena, California, was a partnership with Bill Graves, but in 1951 it split, and I went to work for my dad full-time. My dad passed away in 1976, and I kept it going. In the early '80s, business was down and the Factory wanted me to move into a larger building. I couldn't see starting over at the age of 53, so I decided to shut down the dealership.

Early bob-jobs from the '20s.

At about that time a guy named Jack Malone had the fleet center job, and he was about to leave.

Editor's note: The fleet center is a grouping of new Harley-Davidson models available to magazine editors, journalists of every type worldwide, celebrities, and dignitaries for loan. These bikes are worked hard and put away wet on a general basis, which is expected. It was and is the fleet center manager's job to uncrate, set up, break in, allot, and maintain these new motorcycles. It's a solitary job of tremendous responsibility.

Buzz Buzzelli worked at the Factory then, and he called me about the opening. I applied for the job and got it. I took it over in 1984 with the beginning of the Evolution engine. It's interesting to note that the entire time I ran the fleet center I never had to work on an engine, except to reseal a couple of rocker covers. Jack did plenty of engine work on Shovels due to quality problems and the material change required to run unleaded fuels, but I never had to, and I had to deal with a lot more bikes over the last 15 years. I took the job in April of 1984. I never expected to get the job, but I thoroughly enjoyed every day.

In 1998 the Factory was going to increase the fleet and procure a larger facility. Instead they hired a contractor to take on the larger fleet. I sort of worked myself out of a job. There was plenty to do in Milwaukee, but I wasn't about to pick up roots at this stage of my life and go to Milwaukee, so I retired.

What do you plan to do with your retirement?

I have about two thirds of a 1910 Harley to put together. I have the hard parts: the engine, the pulleys, the fenders, the frame, the handlebars, and the front forks. When I got the front end, they had bent the crap out of the forks to attach a plow bolted to the front fender; the handlebars were jammed on the fork; and it had a rusty wheel without the tire. They're straight, but somewhat rough. So I'll be tinkering with older bikes.

Tell us the story about your father in the '30s and his struggle to keep his dealership alive during the Great Depression.

It was in 1932 when my dad and his partner took all the cash out of the dealership with the exception of $1.75 between them. At the time, that was enough to buy an armload of groceries. They put all the money in a night deposit at the bank and went home. That was on a Saturday night. They came back on Monday and the bank was closed and never opened again. That was a common occurrence during the '30s. Friends heard that Bill and Chubby were in trouble and they came in and paid the money they owed, and some others even paid some money they didn't owe, just to keep them going. A couple of weeks later, Arthur Davidson called and said, 'Chub, I heard the bank closed. Is that right?' My dad said, 'Yep.'

'Well, there's two motorcycles and a box of parts on the way,' Arthur said.

115

Bruce Chubbuck

'I can't pay for 'em,' my dad said.
Arthur said, 'Some day you'll sell the sonuvabitches, then you'll pay for 'em.'
During the Depression, instead of firing employees, the Factory cut the employees' time back so they could all stay employed. They started working on the '36 61-inch in 1932. In 1934 they almost scrapped the Knuckle, but they kept plodding along until finally they shipped 'em. At the time H-D also was taking on outside contract work for extra income.

The '40s were the war years. Could you tell me a story that would be indicative of the era, the people, and the Harley business?

The new '42s came out in September, then Pearl Harbor happened. After Pearl Harbor, everything was restricted. They were shipping a few bikes to dealerships mainly for police departments and WLAs to the front for the military throughout the war, and the Factory kept building until the time when the restrictions would be lifted. They built over 60,000 '45s for the war effort. We had new bikes immediately after the war, in the fall of 1945.

In the '50s you worked for the dealership. What occurred to make that era distinctive?

During the Thanksgiving week of 1951 in Milwaukee, Harley-Davidson unveiled the new K-model to the dealers. We discovered that they were pressing the flywheels together mechanically. No tapers, keys, or nuts. They had some bikes on display, and all dealers had the opportunity to ride them. In the process they shifted the flywheels. They wouldn't hold, and the Factory blamed it on the California dealers. They were forced to uncrate every K-model and replace the flywheels, but they were still on the dealer floors in January.

You read in the history books about K-models only doing 90 mph, but I knew of several that would run over 100.

Did the '50s mark the beginning of the chopper?

No. There were always choppers, but they called 'em bob-jobs. My dad's partner had a flat-tank JD that was chopped. He shortened the bars, took the front fender off, and replaced it with an alloy job from a car tire cover. He also took the hinge pin out of the rear fender, removing the rear third of the fender, then moving the stand clip from the bottom of the fender to the top to hold the jiffy stand.

Was there something about the industry in the '50s that sticks out in your mind?

The worst thing that happened was the movie The Wild Ones. That made us the bad guys. Johnson Motors in Pasadena (Ariel and Triumph distributor) had Hollywood investors. Pete Colman, [the] general manager, called me and told me about the proposed movie. He asked me to contact Walter Davidson. Walter got together with the AMA and had a meeting with the studio. They agreed to modify the script and everyone was happy. However, they ultimately produced the movie as originally planned. Even though Marlon Brando rode a Triumph on a regular basis and in the movie, the movie was bad for the entire industry.

That brings us to the wild '60s. What was your role at the dealership during that period?

There was a rumor out in the middle '60s that the company was almost broke. That was when they put stock on the market for the first time. If you're going bankrupt you can't issue stock. You also can't buy Americhi in Italy, and that deal was put together in 1959. The reason they issued stock in the mid '60s was that the tooling was wearing out and to some extent they were losing their tolerances. There was also a rumor that Ford was going to build a motorcycle. It turned out Ford thought it could buy Harley-Davidson. The Factory told Ford that H-D was not for sale and that was the end of that. But the rumor was out there that Ford was going to build a motorcycle. They had the bucks to do it, and we didn't need that.

The '70s marked the era of the

Bruce Chubbuck setting off on a road trip.

Shovelhead. What were you doing during that decade, and how did the Shovelhead impact your business?

During the late '70s, the biggest problem was the top ends and the sticking valves due to the change in fuels. In 1981, Harley-Davidson got the valves straightened out. I came in at just the right time, with the Evolution change.

An investment company perked up its ears also during that era, not knowing that Ford was not a player, and raided H-D stock, running the price up to $42 a share. H-D looked for a conglomerate and decided to merge with AMF, who was big enough that the raiders were no longer a problem.

The rumor has always been that AMF was responsible for the cheapening of Harleys. It was actually the AMF management team that bought the company. AMF thought that due to the cost of gas, they could sell thousands of inexpensive motorcycles for basic transportation. But the auto industry kept up with the gas crisis by building more fuel-efficient products, so our motorcycle market never boomed and AMF lost interest. AMF put $3–$12 million a year into Harley-Davidson tooling. E. Gus Davis, president of H-D for AMF, said in 1973 that it was better that AMF take the bad PR for the downturn in Harley-Davidson quality, so if they parted ways the stinky reputation went with AMF and didn't stick to the Factory.

That's when Vaughn Bealls, Willie G., John Davidson, and others got together to buy the company back in a leveraged buyout, but ultimately John Davidson opted out.

The '80s were a boom decade for the Factory with the move to go public and the introduction of the Evolution. But you made the decision to close your dealership. How did you feel at the time? What did you think you would do?

It was a tough decision, to close the dealership, which took over a year to make. With all the bullshit involved in running the day-to-day operations of a business, it wasn't fun anymore. Then in April I got a call from Buzz Buzzelli and my whole world changed. I got to work and ride on really new bikes. I was in Harley Heaven!

The '90s marked another decade of involvement in the industry, but also another turning point. You worked closely with the Evolution from start to finish. How did you see it progress?

From the Factory standpoint, the '80s marked the beginning of the best era for quality, and now it gets better every year, including the new 88-inch driveline and the new Softail.

How long were you involved with the stunt team? How did you get involved, and where did it take you?

In the summer of 1978 the Victor McLaglen Motorcorps was turned over to Harry Fisher, an old friend. He was looking for bodies and he invited me to join in, and I've been there ever since. Victor was an Academy Award–winning actor who had developed several drill teams. He had the Light Horse Brigade, the Flying Corps, and a nurses corps for parades and special events. The bike team was originally started in 1935 at Rich Budelier's Harley-Davidson in downtown Los Angeles. The dealership didn't have the money to run it during the Depression, so the guys went to Victor, who turned them down—until they challenged him. If they could do all the stunts the horses did, would he take them on? They did, and he kept his word. Initially the bike team was used as an escort team for special occasions. Victor passed away some 20 years ago.

We are interviewing Harry Fisher next to capture the long history of the Victor McLaglen drill team and its members. Watch for it in the next issue. **HRB**

Appendix C

Captain Truman (Nick) Ward DeRush

In addition to being the first leader of the Victor McLaglen Motor Corps, which was created in1935, it was Nick who convinced movie actor, Victor McLaglen, to sponsor his team of stunt motorcycle riders.

Nick was born in Colorado on October 3, 1908. His given name was Truman Ward DeRush and his nickname was Nick. Whether he chose "Nick" as a Hollywood stage name for his career as a stuntman is unknown. What is known is he was called "Nick" by everyone thereafter.

Nick and his wife, Eunice, were married in Los Angeles, California on July 13, 1929 and they had four sons: (1) Truman Leon, (2) Don Lee, (3) Gilbert "Duke" Ray, and (4) Damon "Rocky."

During a conversation with Duke, I discovered Nick endured multiple challenges and hardships in his life. One of the more interesting was that he had polio as a child which left him with temporary paralysis on one half of his body. It's amazing to think he was able to overcome this handicap and become a motorcycle stuntman responsible for the establishment of a Motor Corps which is still active today.

There are quite a few stories about Nick and, of course, the good ones are all true. One such story speaks to Nick's weekend escapades to Santa Monica, California. It seems he and his buddies would go to the Santa Monica Pier and hang out while Nick would ride his bike out to the end of the pier. (Of course, you can't do that nowadays, but -- in the 1930s, apparently you could.) This motorcycle ride to the end of the pier captured everyone's attention and, pretty soon, the excitement drew quite a crowd. Once the gathering grew large enough, Nick's buddies would start passing around the hat. Anyone who wanted to see Nick ride his motorcycle off the end of the pier and splash into the water just needed to put some money in the hat. Once enough money had been collected (and I have no idea how much that would have been), Nick fired up his Harley to get set for this magnificent feat. He'd race back and forth a few times to get the crowd going. Then, he'd rev the bike, pick up speed, and ride off the end of the pier and into the Pacific Ocean. His buddies would gather up the money, help Nick fish himself and his motorcycle out of the salt water, and haul the bike back to the shop. They'd work all week getting the motorcycle dried out. They had to remove the salt from the carburetor, engine, pistons, gas tank, fuel lines, and every other nook and cranny. By the time the next weekend came around, Nick, his bike and his buddies were ready to rush back to the pier, so they could do it all over again. This occurred weekend after weekend unless, of course, the group had a Motor Corps' show scheduled.

We're pretty sure the Santa Monica pier story is true because of our sources. It was told by an "old timer" at one of the teams' banquets, and it was told again from a complete outsider, who said his dad worked for the movie industry at the time and had told him the same story. Well, in hard times, you gotta do what you gotta do to make a few bucks!

Santa Monica Pier - built in 1909

***Pictures and information from
https://www.santamonicapier.org/history***

In 1919, the pier collapsed and was rebuilt. In 1924. it was *". . . sold to a local concern called the Santa Monica Amusement Company. The new company quickly upgraded the roller coaster and the new Whirlwind Dipper – a longer, faster coaster designed by renowned Prior & Church Company. Next, they began work on a ballroom – the largest in the world."*

Nick passed on January 6, 1962 in Fontana, California. When I was doing research for my book, *The Amazing Victor McLaglen Motor Corps*, I discovered Nick was buried at Inglewood Park Cemetery in Inglewood, California.

So, one sunny day, we took a motorcycle ride to the cemetery to take a look. Much to my surprise, Nick was in an unmarked grave. Now, that just didn't seem right! Was it possible the founder of the Victor McLaglen Motor Corps and the leader of our famous motorcycle stunt team was laid to rest in the grass between two, unrelated gravestone markers? That sent me on a quest to rectify the situation and provide Truman Ward (Nick) DeRush with a gravestone worthy of his contributions to the Corps.

 A discussion with the VMMC team members proved everyone was onboard, so I continued my investigation. I recalled I had received a message from Don Carlos DeRush from Pasadena, California, identifying himself as one of Nick's grandsons. He had read my book and was reaching out to see if I had more photos of his grandfather, Nick. He was unaware his grandfather had no gravestone and he was surprised. I shared with him the VMCC's wish to honor his grandfather with a marker and promised to keep in touch.

Well, COVID-19 hit our country with full force and I was unable to make much progress with this project for much of a full year. Eventually, however, progress was again established and we were making some headway. Father Frank used a bit of influence and was able to obtain funding from a local charity to get the stone engraved, we obtained permission from the family (Don) to go forth with the plan, and Father Frank then coordinated with the cemetery administration office for payment and placement of the new stone.

Finally, the stone was installed and we were able to plan a blessing ceremony commemorating placement of the engraved gravestone in Nick's honor.

Inglewood Park Cemetery
720 E Florence Avenue
Inglewood, California 90301

The following invitation to the ceremony was emailed to members of the Corps, friends and family, and Nick's grandson, Don.

> *Truman (Nick) Ward DeRush passed away on January 6, 1962. As you may know, Nick was vital to the establishment of the Victor McLaglen Motor Corps in 1935.*
>
> *Nick was interred in Inglewood Park Cemetery and the Motor Corps has recently produced an engraved stone to mark his final resting place.*
>
> *You are invited to attend a brief ceremony to bless this new engraved marker at the gravesite. As proud members of the Motor Corps, family and friends, we hope you will attend this tribute to a key founding member.*
>
> *March 20, 2022 at 10:00 a.m.*
> *Father Frank Hicks to Officiate the Ceremony*

Don Carlos DeRush (Nicky's grandson) called his father; Gilbert "Duke" DeRush; and his uncle, Damon "Rocky" DeRush to tell them what was happening and on March 20, 2022, they, and more than 20 people, arrived at the cemetery to show their respects. The team was proud to have Father Frank Hicks (a long-time member of the VMMV) preside over the ceremony.

Duke, Don and Rocky DeRush   **Gravestone**

   Father Frank introduced the Motor Corps members and guests, a few words were spoken by the participants, and Father Frank gave the blessing and benediction. Afterward, we all met at a member's home for refreshments and reminiscing.

   We -- as Motor Corps members, past members and retirees – are very proud of the Victor McLaglen Motor Corps and owe a debt of gratitude to Captain DeRush for his role in creating, leading and promoting our world famous motorcycle stunt team.

   Finally, it was our pleasure and honor to provide a gravestone to mark Nicky's final resting place.

   After several communications with Nick DeRush's grandson, Don Carlos DeRush, I now plan to visit Trona, CA where Nick grew up and where his mom ran a café. It looks like an interesting little place to visit.

Appendix D

Fred H. Fahnestock

Fred was 104 years old when he passed away. I have included Fred's Obituary, not only because he was a former Motor Corps member, but because I think he is was just a very interesting guy who had a very interesting life.

"Obituary," The Village News - Fallbrook & Bansall (http://www.villagenew.com/obituaries) Fred Fahnestock, died 25 October 2018."

Fred Hannibal Fahnestock passed away peacefully in his home with his son, H. James Fahnestock (Jim), and his caregiver, Rose Padong, by his side on October 25, going to join his wife of 75 years in heaven with the Lord.

Fred was born the third of four children (two brothers and one sister) to Fred Sr. and Birdy Fahnestock in Villa Grove, Illinois on January 9, 1914. He is survived by his two sons, Fred M. Fahnestock (Freddie) and Jim Fahnestock, five grandchildren, and a multitude of great-grandchildren and extended family.

After moving to Los Angeles, California in 1937, Fred met Jessie Mae Brooks, the love of his life, and they wed in 1938. They were married for 75 years until Jessie's passing in 2013.

Fred started his career as a salesman for a Pontiac dealership in downtown Los Angeles, where the Staples Center now stands. During this time, he was also a charter member of the Victor McLaglen (sic) Light Horse and rode in the motorcycle stunt and drill team. After five years at the Pontiac dealership, Fred signed up for the Army Air Corps to fight in World War II.

He served his country as a tail gunner in a B-24 Liberator, 8th Air Force, 258th Bomber Group. He flew 31 missions over Europe, reached the rank of Staff Sergeant and received the Distinguished Flying Cross, in addition to other awards. Though Fred served in many B-24s during the course of the war, he flew his final missions aboard the Stardust where, in honor of his wife, he emblazoned the name "Jessie Mae" on the tail next to where he manned the twin 50 caliber guns.

After returning from the war, Fred and Jessie settled in South Gate, Calif., where they raised their two sons, and Fred resumed working at the same Pontiac dealership in L.A. They lived there for 30 years before moving to Lake Forest, Calif.

In 1956, Fred began working in Pasadena, Calif. as a civilian employee for the U.S. Army in procurement for their missile division. After 25 years, he retired in 1981 at the age of 67.

In 2001, Fred and Jessie moved to Fallbrook to be closer to their son, Jim. Both were members of the United Methodist Church and active in the community. Jessie belonged to the Fallbrook Women's Club while Fred served as a member of Toastmasters.

Fred
USAF Tailgunner

Fred was a natural storyteller who would often spin tales from his own life (with varying degrees of embellishment) and capture audiences with his favorite jokes. At 104 years old, Fred outlived every single one of his friends from his old neighborhoods and all of his relatives aside from his children.

But while living in Fallbrook, he developed a new circle of friends which gathered together the Friday after his passing to toast his rich and full life. His friends regaled each other with the many interesting stories Fred had told them over the years, remembering to throw in an off-color joke or two, which is exactly the way Fred would have wanted it.

There will be no service other than the spreading of Fred's and Jessie's ashes at sea, where they will be together forever.

Appendix E

Harry M. Fisher

As a young lad, Harry attended several public schools in the San Fernando area before he was kicked out for "who-knows-what" reason. He was then sent to the Mount Lowe Military Academy in Altadena, California. His dad thought the academy might "straighten him out," but it didn't. Finally, he transferred to Hollywood Professional School (HPS). Harry's mother had attended HPS and his grandmother worked at the school as an art teacher. The school catered to students/ entertainers who needed to attend school, but also had "call times" dictated by the movie studios. HPS was a perfect fit for Harry and he got along with the other students, who were in the entertainment business. Notable celebrities such as singer Brenda Lee, actress Lauren Chapin of *Father Knows Best,* and Mouseketeers Cubby O'Brien and Annette Funicello were just a few of the students who attended while Harry was a student. He did not know them all, but he did mention he and Lauren Chapin often got in trouble in class. I can believe this!

It was during his education at HPS that Harry learned about showmanship and gained his "the show must go on" attitude. It was these formidable years which built a perfect foundation for Harry to lead the VMMC and Huntington Park Elks teams.

Following graduation from HPS, Harry attended Los Angeles City College, where he majored in Police Science and played defensive positions on their water polo team. His mother, Ruth Elaine Fisher, was employed by the Los Angeles Police Department and rode a three-wheel motorcycle to work. At one time, Harry thought he might follow in her footsteps and get into law enforcement.

1965 Water Polo Team
Los Angeles City College

Harry's Mom, Ruth
Meter Maid
Los Angeles Police Department

It's entirely possible Harry's attraction to motorcycles was genetic. After all, his mother, Ruth Elaine (Sorenson) Fisher and her brother, "Uncle" Harry Sorenson, were avid motorcyclists. At 5'2" and about 105 lbs., Harry's mom could outride most any big, burly biker, except her brother and she really tried to outdo him, too! She had also attended and graduated from HPS and had aspired to become an actress. Although there were some promising offers, Ruth gave up her dream and took a job at Stationer's Corporation in Los Angeles where she rode throughout downtown Los Angeles delivering products on a 3-wheel motorcycle. Ruth eventually gained employment with the Los Angeles Police Department where she worked as a Meter Maid on another 3-wheel motorcycle until her retirement.

Harry's Mom
Stationer's Corporation Rig
Los Angeles, California

Ruth's Headshot

Harry's Mom, Ruth
1959 FL Harley

Harry's love of motorcycles began as a young boy and lasted throughout adulthood. He also enjoyed watching them race, but his real passion was when he was the one doing the racing. Harry decided he wanted to race motorcycles at Ascot Raceway (now defunct). He even had someone who agreed to help him get his start. When his mother heard of his plan, she knew she had to create a diversion/alternative to prevent her son from the dangers of racing. It was at this time (age 15) that she introduced him to Herb Harker, the leader of the Victor McLaglen Motor Corps, and urged Herb to allow her son to join the team.

Los Angeles Speedway opened in 1957, on the site of a former city dump. It was built less than 1 mile from the former site of Carrell Speedway, which had been closed in late 1954 to make way for the Artesia Fwy. The track was renamed to New Ascot Stadium in October 1958 as part of a management change. The track assumed the name it held until its closure, Ascot Park in 1961. J. C. Agajanian promoted major races at the venue, and later leased the track from 1976 until his death in 1984, when his family continued operating the venue. His radio advertisements ended with the phrase 'Come to Ascot, where the 110, the 405 and the 91 freeways collide!'".
Wikipedia. 2022. "Ascot Park." Wikimedia Foundation. 24 March 2022.

This alternative plan worked until Harry was in his early 20s and no longer living with his mom. He still had the "biker bug" to compete, and he started racing sidehacks. A racing sidehack is a motorcycle with a sort of platform and third wheel attached to the side of the bike. It took a driver and a passenger (monkey) -- who rode on the platform -- to balance the vehicle around corners and maneuver jumps. Initially, Harry was the monkey. When he got his own sidehack, the positions changed and he graduated to the driver's position having many unsuspecting new passengers take on the role of the monkey.

*Driver: **Harry Fisher***
*Monkey: **Ronnie Smith***

One of Harry's many, varied professions included a stint with the Rapid Blue Print Company as a motorcycle and van deliverer/"shagger" of blueprints. (Notice whatever form of employment he had, there was always a bike involved.) His work transportation was a 1964 "shag" bike, the very one used for the Motor Corps.

Harry Fisher   ***Rapid Blue Print Company***
"Shag" Bike

In his capacity as a van/delivery driver for the Rapid Blue Print Company, he was a staunch member of the Teamsters Union. When the union was on strike, Harry supported the membership with his picket sign and had great fun participating!

Teamsters Strike 1966
L-R: Tom Davies, Mozie, Harry Fisher, Rod Byerly, Dave Bird

When I first started dating Harry in 1966, he was developing a circus act with his good friend, wing-walker Johnny Kazian and then-wife, Terri. Their plan was to do all the stunts they could possibly conjure up, using Harry and Johnny's Harley-Davidson motorcycles, and perform all of the stunts in a 50-foot circle (a requirement for all three-ring circus acts). Johnny was also a VMMC member.

Harry (Motorman) and Terri on Bike
Johnny on Ladder

Motorman: Harry Fisher *Motorman: Harry Fisher*
Top: Johnny and Terri *Standing: Johnny Kazian*
  Tom: Terri Kazian

Their costumes included silky, baby-blue colored shirts and black pants. I don't know exactly what happened, but they didn't "run away to the circus!" I think they may have started questioning themselves when Harry and Johnny were developing their wing-walking act with a motorcycle-to-biplane transfer on a swinging ladder. It's a mystery to me why, at that time, I didn't start questioning my intelligence in dating this guy! My mother definitely didn't know about all this or I probably would have been immediately shipped back home to Maine!

In the early 1970s, Harry decided he needed to make more money, so he went to truck driving school and received his Commercial Driver's License (CDL). He then quit Rapid Blue Print Company and went to work for Hadley Auto Transport delivering new Ford cars throughout California, Arizona and Nevada. Harry continued to lead the Huntington Park Elks Motorcycle Stunt and Drill Team until around 1975 when he quit Hadley Auto Transport, moved to Sylmar, California and started the San Fernando Motorcycle Repair Shop business with a partner. Harry had little idle time and – with a wife and baby to support – he worked as a motorcycle funeral escort during the day and at the motorcycle shop in the evening. Harry's busy schedule required he take a couple of years off from the Elks team.

A request from Herb Harker to assume his position as Colonel of the VMMC (so he could retire and move to Illinois), prompted Harry to disband his motorcycle repair business. He continued his funeral escort business, bought and managed J. C. Armature (rebuilding and shipping motorcycle armatures and field coils across the U.S.), and he relocated to Cerritos, California with his wife and son.

At the peak of his escort business, Harry had about 35 funeral business accounts and a dozen or so escorts who worked for him. Harry maintained this business until 2012 when he sold it to Judy Green, who had worked as his dispatcher and office manager.

Around 1990, Brenda Solarzano Harry started up a company called Partners Limousine Service. The name changed a few times (V.I.P. Limousine Service, then All Cities Limousine Service). Harry and Brenda ran this limo service while Harry continued the funeral escort business. Of course, he also had his VMMC meetings, practices and performances which were often held in the business parking lot. Many of the escort riders would ride their motorcycles for funerals in the morning, then chauffeur the limousines in the afternoon. Some would even participate with the motorcycle team.

V.I.P. Limousine Company
Pico Rivera, California

Patches

Harry found Patches in a gutter outside the V.I.P. Limousine Company office during a rain storm. She was wet, cold, skinny, and definitely in need of some loving care. Harry brought her inside, dried her off, and gave her a little food and water. She quickly curled up and went to sleep on the couch. We tried to find her rightful owners, but to no avail. We decided she was ours to keep. Harry would set her on the seat of the motorcycle and she'd stay there until he returned. He would sit her in front of him on the bike and she'd just lean into him to enjoy the ride. She was very trusting.

Harry and Patches were inseparable and were often seen riding the bike together. Patches went everywhere with Harry, and she was a real asset in gaining attention and popularity at the shows; especially with the children.

In 1981, Harry received a call from Metro-Goldwyn-Mayer (MGM). They were looking for a stuntman to act as Erik Estrada's double for the television series, CHIPS. (Erik starred in this series along with Larry Wilcox.) The studio wanted someone who could do motorcycle stunts and had heard Harry was the leader of just such a group of riders.

This sounded like a lot of fun, so Harry called in sick at work several days in a row and took the job!

"Yep, I've got the CHP uniform and I'm ready to go!"

Photo Licensed by CC-BY-NC

"I've got the official CHP helmet – Lookin' good!"

"Got the black 'Estrada' Wig"

Harry also lead the team in the 1971 movie, *Evel Knievel*, starring George Hamilton.

More photos from CHIPS.

"Floorboard Ride"
Harry as Eric Estrada

"Side Ride"
Harry as Eric Estrada

Harry and Erik getting ready to ride

In 2007, Harry had the good fortune to work on the American biker comedy film, *Wild Hogs,* starring Tim Allen, John Travolta, Martin Lawrence, and William H. Macy. It just so happens, it was filmed in Santa Fe, New Mexico where Harry and I would buy a home and where we would eventually retire. Back to the movie . . .

Harry was charged with responsibility for the actors' motorcycles. This included ensuring the bikes were on the set and ready to go when they were needed. He said it was great fun and made us all anxious to see the movie as soon as it was released.

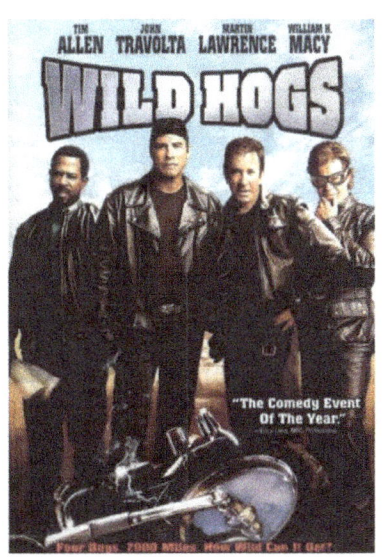

Appendix F

Marty Fisher

Marty's article for Honda Rider's Club Association (HRCA) quarterly publication to their members

GROWING UP IN THE MOTOR CORPS

My interest in motorcycles goes all the way back to early October 1974 as a 10-day-old newborn in Southern California. That day, my dad sat on his motorcycle and held me in his arms. That does not seem like the safest thing to do with a newborn, but if you knew my dad, you would completely understand. My dad comes from a family with deep motorcycle roots dating back to the 1940s. He grew up with his mom and uncle teaching him how to ride. By 15, he was tearing around Los Angeles, riding his motorcycle to school and wherever else he needed to go. Later he used his motorcycle to make money, working as a courier for a blueprint company in downtown Los Angeles and as a funeral motorcycle escort.

This was what he did for a living, but his real interest was in racing. As a teenager though, his mom didn't want him to race because it was dangerous (the mom mantra). Instead of racing, she encouraged him to get involved with a precision slow-speed motorcycle stunt and drill team, the Victor McLaglen Motor Corps. She believed that the team would help him improve his skills, make him a better rider in a supervised environment and keep him out of trouble! Not only did he become a better rider, he became the leader in 1978. He has been with the team for more than 40 years, taking them from coast to coast to entertain thousands at events such as Daytona Bike Week, Lake George and the Torrance Ride for Kids.

Most kids have to talk their parents into buying them a motorcycle. Luckily, this wasn't the case for me. My dad bought me a used 1969 Honda Trail 50 from a friend before I was even old enough to touch the ground. At about 5 years old, I was finally able to ride it myself and my dad would take me to the Motor Corps practice field, a wide-open parking lot, and send me off to ride around for hours at a time. I can't tell you how many Sundays I spent in parking lots riding my "bike." We would also head out to the Southern California desert for an occasional dirt-bike ride

Above: Marty (right) and his dad enjoying the view on the Blue Ridge Parkway during the Honda Hoot. Below: Marty (bottom, right) and his dad (bottom, second from left) performing with the Victor McLaglen Motor Corps during the Ride for Kids event in Torrance, California.

on my Honda XR75. My dad also did some local flat-track and side-hack racing. Although I was too young to remember it, the pictures sure are cool! My family always liked to go to the dirt-track races at Ascot in Gardena, California. I remember watching Bubba Shobert and Ricky Graham in the '80s on their Honda RS750 flat-trackers winning national championships.

At age 15, I joined the Victor McLaglen Motor Corps. I learned how to become a better rider with my dad teaching me the insider tips and techniques to improve my skills. I was always told that anybody can twist the throttle and ride fast, but going slow was even harder. (Remember taking the taking the DMV motorcycle riding test as a beginning rider?) What better way to go to motorcycle events all over the country for free and perform in front of other motorcyclists?

While in college I was able to keep riding with the team and also worked at a motorcycle dealership. After traveling to many major events, including Lake George, Sturgis and more than 20 International Motorcycle Shows, I realized how much I wanted to make my career in the motorcycle industry. As luck would have it, the Motor Corps was performing at the Ride for Kids at the Honda Headquarters in Torrance, California. That is where I met my future boss, Charlie Keller, for the first time. I couldn't think of a better place to work in the industry than for Honda. A position became available and I've been working for the HRCA for more than four years now.

While riding around in parking lots as a kid, or even in college, I would have never thought that riding motorcycles would turn into a career with Honda!

■ *Marty Fisher*
HRCA Western Regional Representative

Appendix G

Fr. Francis (Frank) Hicks

Frank's life has been blessed with a myriad of professions, careers and international travel. As newsman, Paul Harvey, was prone to say, here's the "rest of the story ..." as told by Frank, himself.

"I was born August 6, 1941 in Providence, Rhode Island. I attended local parochial schools, Providence Country Day Preparatory School, and graduated from Providence College in June 1963 with a Bachelor of Arts in Political Science. I attended the University of Rhode Island graduate school from 1963-65.

In October 1965, I was selected as a Peace Corps volunteer for service in Thailand and was assigned, after language and cultural training, to Srisaket Province in the northeast of Thailand as a Community Development Volunteer where I served until February 1969.

Following my return to the United States in 1969, I received an appointment as a Patrol Agent with the United States Border Patrol stationed at Fort Hancock, Texas El Paso Sector (1970). In November 1971, I transferred to the Criminal Investigations Branch of the United States Immigration Service at the Los Angeles District. I served as Special Agent, Prosecutions Officer (Los Angeles District) as well as the permanent service representative on the Drug Enforcement Agency's task force.

Because of my language skills and interpreter rating in the Thai-Lao language, I was detailed to work as the United States Immigration Examiner in the refuge camps in South East Asia (1978). In 1983, I was appointed Assistant District Director for Detention and Deportation for the Los Angeles District. In 1985, I transferred to the Regional Officer of the Immigration Service as the Deputy to the Assistant Western Regional Commissioner for Criminal Investigations.

During my tenure at the regional headquarters, I was assigned as Coordinator for the Office of Internal Investigations, as well as the Immigration Representative on the National Narcotic Border Interdiction Systems led by the U.S. Coast Guard under the direction of the Office of the Vice President of the United States, George Bush. In 1991, I was attached to the United States Attorney's Office Central District of California as the immigration representative for organized crime and racketeering and was a designated prosecution agent for the Immigration Service under the RICO statutes. My area of primary responsibility was dealing with Asian organized crime and smuggling elements and the so-called Russian mafia associations.

In June 1993, I retired completing a 23-year career with the Department of Justice, Immigration and Naturalization Service.

Following a year (1993-1994) of spiritual discernment at St. Gregory's Benedictine Abbey in Shawnee, Oklahoma, I entered St. John's Seminary at Camarillo, California (August 1995) to study for the priesthood. I graduated from St. John's in December 1999 with a Master in Divinity, as well as a Master of Arts in Theology and Church History.

I was ordained to the priesthood by Cardinal Roger Mahoney on January 15, 2000 for the Archdiocese of Los Angeles and was assigned to Holy Trinity Parish in San Pedro, California as an associate pastor.

In the Spring of 2001, I was appointed a chaplain and special reserve officer with the Los Angeles Police Department and the Critical Incident Response Team. I am also a supply chaplain certified to the Federal Correctional Center,

(L-R) Fr. Truc Nguyen Cardinal Mahoney. Fr. Frank at the Ordination

Terminal Island, California; and chaplain of the Victor McLaglen Motor Corps. I also serve as a Board member and Vice President of FedOne Federal Credit Union and McIntyre House Recovery Center. I am a member of the Benevolent Order of Elks and a Knight Commander of the Equestrian Order of the Holy Sepulcher of Jerusalem.

On July 1, 2004, I was assigned as associate pastor at St. Mel's parish in Woodland Hills, California. In 2006, I was appointed administrator of the St. Basil's parish in Los Angeles and, in 2008, installed as pastor of St. Basil's by Bishop Edward Clarke.

In 2009, I was appointed by Cardinal Mahoney as Director of the Cardinal McIntyre Fund for Charity. In August 2011, Archbishop Gomez asked that I serve as Associate Vicar for Clergy for a period of one year while major changes were developed within that office. I returned to the Cardinal McIntyre Fund as Director on July 1, 2012."

"I am presently assigned as chaplain for the Olympic Division Los Angeles Police Department (LAPD) and denominational specific (Roman Catholic) for the entire LAPD, and serve on the Chaplain's Advisory Board for the Chief of Police, Chaplain to the Los Angeles Policy Emerald Society and a Board member of the Desert Refuge Retreat Center in Joshua Tree, California -- serving both police and active military personnel. I am also a long-time platelet donor at the City of Hope Cancer Center in Duarte, California. Recently, I accepted the position as volunteer on-call night duty chaplain for the Emergency Room at Cedars-Sinai Hospital in Los Angeles.

I have also served as a member of the Archdiocesan Clergy Personnel Board (2005-2008) and the Archdiocesan Health Program (2011-2012) under the auspices of the RETA (Anthem Blue Cross).

In 2004, I received Alumni of the Year Award from Providence College and, in 2006, I received The St. Michael's Award as the outstanding Chaplain of the Los Angeles Police Department. I have also been awarded membership in the St. Dominic Society of Providence College for significant financial support of the college. I am also a member of the Friends of St. John's Seminary. In the 2012 Providence College Fall Quarterly, I was featured in the cover article and have been asked to be the after-dinner speaker for the 50th Reunion for the Class of 1963 celebration. In 2013, I was selected by the Los Angeles Archdiocese as one of the 12 outstanding persons in the Archdiocese."

St. Basil Catholic Church
3611 Wilshire Blvd, Los Angeles, CA

Finally, Father Frank enjoys his leisure time as much as his work. His hobbies include motorcycling (Harley-Davidson, of course), music, reading, stamp collecting, traveling, cooking, raising orchids and gardening in general.

Appendix H

Bob Holbrook

Hot Rod Bike magazine, "Bruce Chubbuck" (Kendall, K.R., June 2000)
EDSG company newspaper, "Real People: Bob Holbrook" (Lahnala, D.).

EDSG's Real People: Bob Holbrook

Daredevils Bob Holbrook and Evel Knievel have two things in common: they both like motorcycle stunts and flashy uniforms. Holbrook, a data processing analyst at Hughes, belongs to the Victor McLaglen Motor Corps Motorcycle Stunt and Drill Team.

Though Holbrook, who lives in West L.A., said he prefers silver embellishments and stars, the Motor Corps presently dresses in dark brown uniforms similar to the California Highway Patrol's garb. Add a white helmet and a black and white Harley Davidson, and Holbrook looks convincingly like a bona fide cop.

"I'll be riding to a performance and someone will say, 'Hey officer, how do I get to the parade?' Sometimes I go ahead and give directions and they never realize I'm just an ordinary citizen."

Holbrook got involved with the "bike" club about a year ago. Since then he's learned 12 stunts, to which there are basically three aspects: driving, supporting, and the daredevil stuff – such as standing on the supporter's shoulders. All the tricks are done while moving at an average speed of 10 miles per hour.

"The most dangerous stunt I've done is the 'Standing Horse,'" he said. "In it, I leap on the back of a bike as another team member drives by. Then, as we're moving, I climb on top of his shoulders and stand up, holding onto a rope attached to the handlebars."

In addition to stunts, the team performs precision riding – figure eights, crossovers and other, more elaborate routines.

Holbrook performed in about 40 parades this year, including the Hollywood Santa Claus Lane Parade. Most of his weekends are spent practicing for or riding in performances. The Motor Corps has appeared at the San Francisco Cow Palace, the Las Vegas Helldorado Days, and just recently at a Fourth of July spectacular in Cerritos. This September they will be featured in a "That's Incredible" segment filmed at the Ventura Motorcycle Jamboree on Memorial Day weekend.

The club currently has 30 members. For more information, contact Bob Holbrook, Culver City, ext. 7184, or Harry Fisher, the corps commander, at 792-1300.

– Dinah Lahnala

Bob Holbrook (top) and fellow motor corps member Chuck Buckner demonstrate the "Standing Horse" stunt.

Appendix I

John (Johnny) Mark Kazian

Johnny Kazian Performs in The Great Waldo Pepper

Johnny had quite an interesting career in "wingwalking. In fact, he became known as the "King of the Wingwalkers."

"Obituary," Idaho Statesman (https://www.legacy.com/us/obituaries) Johnny Kazian.

> *"John "Johnny" Kazian, 81, of Kuna, Idaho, fell asleep in the Lord at his home surrounded by family on April 23, 2015. Johnny was born on May 19, 1933 in Philadelphia, Pennsylvania and attended Northeast Public High School and later graduated from Temple University with a degree in mechanical engineering.*
>
> *Johnny lived life to the fullest. In 1947, at the age of 14, he performed as a trapeze artist for the first time after having trained since he was 7. The thrill of "flying through the air" sparked a love for acrobatics that would inspire him to become the greatest wingwalker in the world. Johnny spent his life performing live before thousands of people around the world. Audience members stood and watched in awe as Johnny performed death defying feats such as a plane to plane transfer in mid-air, firewall crashes while hanging from a rope ladder and countless aerobatics while on the wing of the airplane..*

He entertained thousands more as he stunt doubled on numerous television and cinema productions to include television shows such as The Dukes of Hazard, The Six Million Dollar Man and movies such as The Great Waldo Pepper, Capricorn One, The Stuntman and many others.

Though a consummate entertainer, Johnny was also deeply patriotic and answered his country's call to duty on July 24, 1950 when he enlisted in the Navy to fight against the North Koreans. He served honorably and earned many awards and accolades before his discharge on March 18, 1954.

Johnny had many hobbies such as woodworking, land surveying and drawing, but he was most active with the Treasure Valley Pool League. He served as president of the league for over 15 years and greatly looked forward to playing with his team each week.

Johnny was united in marriage to the love of his life, Mary Ellen, on April 23, 1976. He was preceded in death by his father, Nishan Kazian, his mother, Marguerite Maley, and his sister, Mary Feil. He is survived by his wife, Mary Ellen; his daughter, Esther; his son Tony; his grandchildren: Connor, Beck, Myles, Nishan, Kalea and Peyton and his great grandchildren: Bailey and Jamie.

Appendix J

Merideth (Mickey) Minor

This is Mickey's story, as written several years ago.

***Mickey Minor
2006***

"I was standing in front of the drug store with a nickel ice cream cone watching the traffic go through town when I began motorcycle riding in my dreams. Coming into town from either direction was a long downgrade and then a long upgrade out of town. Right in the middle of town was a short dogleg. You could see both ways from the dogleg but traffic had to slow. On the upgrade, riders always seemed to be in a hurry to get out of town. I didn't personally know anyone who rode. Through the years, I met several who said they did, but I never knew anyone with a passion for riding until after I retired from the Navy in 1976 and met Clay Sweeney. Clay was the chairman of the Southern California Motorcycling Association at that time.

Clay told me about a watering hole called the Alpine Inn he used to ride to in Trabuco Canyon. I checked it out and wound up playing music out there for a couple years. More than once on his way home from the Alpine Inn, Clay left his motorcycle in the ditch somewhere and then went back and got it the next day. His wife, Barbara, told him, 'Clay, you've got to quit that before you hurt yourself.' One day, he told me, 'Mickey, I don't think I'll be able to ride out and frolic at the Alpine Inn anymore.'

Clay inspired me and helped me turn my dreams into reality. I got my stuff together, saved some money and paid cash for a new motorcycle. Clay rode it home for me and parked it in my garage. Within a few days, I had my license. By the time I had 60,000 miles on that motorcycle, I had cash to buy another one.

I first heard of the Victor McLaglen Motorcycle Stunt and Drill Team (sic) *at the Motorcycle Jamboree on the fairgrounds at Ventura in 1981. I was playing music on an outdoor bandstand, not far from the arena. I could hear the commotion in the arena Saturday afternoon. I heard later that some guy named Harry Fisher had put his whole team of 23 old goats on one motorcycle and rode around the arena, while 'That's Incredible' filmed it. I went to the arena and watched the show the next day. At dusk with wheel lights on ..."*

"The Victor McLaglen team did a combined show with the Seattle Cossacks from up north. I could tell they were having a lot of fun. I was hooked, but it would still be a while before I learned that the team practiced in Downey.

One Sunday morning in April 1985, I rode to the Elks Lodge parking lot in Downey. Cones were set up and several members were warming up for practice. I talked with team member, Dick Gerry, quite a while before practice. He didn't give me a bit of discouragement, so I submitted my application and then went looking for another motorcycle. This would be my third one.

Production of the 4-speed Harley-Davidson FLH, with the shovelhead engine, ended with the 1984 model, but I finally found a new one in Canoga Park. After I had it painted to specifications, they told me to put the kickstand up and let the motorcycle fall on its left side; then pick it up and let it fall on the right side, and I'd be ready to ride with the team.

I've been riding with the team since April 1985. Over and over, I get 'selected' to go on top of the High Pyramid. We usually end each show with the Pyramid. It's like when the Fat Lady sings! But my favorite stunt is the Wheelbarrow Ride. It has been the most difficult for me to do, both technically and psychologically."

"Wheelbarrow Ride"
Upside Down: Mickey Minor
Rear: Dan Welch

Appendix K

Ray Phillips

Given Name: Raymond Phillips
Date of Birth: March 7, 1903
Place of Birth: Selby Township, Illinois
Siblings: Five (5) Sisters and two (2) Brothers
Father's Profession: Coal Miner and Steam Engineer
Childhood: At 12 years old, Ray went to work on a farm in Illinois.
Employment: Hardware, Plumbing and Brick and Tile.
Past Times: Hunting and Fishing

1925 - Ray and his friend, Mike Clay, bought an old Model T Ford and headed for California
1936 – Ray joined the Motor Corps
1941 – Ray purchased a new Harley and painted it "club" colors
1942 – Ray was drafted into the Army
1947 – Ray earned his pilot's license and purchased a plane

Ray's life story is very interesting and tells about his travels from Illinois to California on unpaved roads, getting that Model T stuck in the mud, hitching rides on trains, and hiding out on those trains to avoid being arrested. Ray and his buddy rode through Yellowstone Park and Montana camping in "potato dugouts," trying to keep dry and warm, and eventually making their way back through Salt Lake City and Las Vegas to end up in California again.

The quotes below are actual excerpts from Ray's personal life experiences (as told in his own words).

"When I was 15, I was talked into boxing. I only fought preliminaries, but due to crooked front teeth and a nose that bled easy, I always looked like I was murdered. So I started wrestling. Well I wasn't getting rich at that and I got tired of having my arms, legs and neck twisted so I quit that nonsense."

". . . I was broke by now and the going really got rough. It was 1929 and no such thing as getting work. Now and then, I would get a meal at some restaurant by washing dishes. I got quite expert at filling my pockets with fruit as I walked through a market. I would start out early in the morning and get a bottle of milk off somebody's porch before they were up. I would get fresh socks and sometimes a clean shirt when someone left their laundry out overnight. I didn't call this stealing. It was simply survival. One time, about six men were working on the highway, they set their lunch

boxes on an embankment while they was working about a half mile down the road. By taking a little out of each box, I had a pretty good lunch and I don't think it hurt them much."

". . . I hitchhiked part of the time and when I thought it advisable, I would catch a freight. You had to be careful back then as they would round up the bums and put them on county work farms for about a month. By keeping in contact with the other bums, I learned what places to avoid and I kept out of trouble."

". . . When it was advisable, I would check into the Police Station and be locked up for the night. You were out of the weather and well accounted for."

". . . As I always had my eye out for something better, I eventually run into a job with the Preston Tire Company at Melrose (Avenue) and Vermont (Avenue). They had a Harley and sidecar I used for pickup and delivery. It wasn't just riding, I also fixed tires till I was black in the face. It was a good job, but I eventually found something better. It was the Velvet Ice Cream Company on East 18th Street."

". . . I was doing good there and could of done better if I had stayed. There was a boyhood friend named Charles Timmerman out here from our home town of Sheffield and we were bumming around together. I let him talk me into a motorcycle trip. Like a fool, I went . . ."

Ray Phillips
Cycle Magazine, March 1951 Issue

If you want to read Ray's entire autobiography, please contact me at rthfisher@gmail.com.

APPENDIX L

Elmer (Hap) Ruggles

Hap left his hometown of Portland, Oregon when he enlisted in the U.S. Navy to support the war effort. Following his service with the Navy, he was employed as a motorcycle officer and a stuntman for the movies. At one time, he even toured with the Al G. Barnes and the Ringling Brothers circuses.

Prior to joining the Victor McLaglen Motor Corps in 1935, he was a drummer with Don Warner's orchestra (popular in the 1920s and 1930s).

When he joined the VMMC, he excelled not only with his expertise in riding a motorcycle, but he was an excellent stuntman and performed feats that no one else thought of, much less would do, riding on a motorcycle.

These lines from George D. Willoughby of Los Angeles, who was watchman of the Rose City Speedway, Portland, Ore, from 1916 to 1923, close the discussion on motor maniacs for the time being: *In the 1940s, George D. Willoughby wrote, "I am reminded that the first to crash a board wall on a motorcycle was done in 1921 on the old Rose City Speedway by Speed Ruggles, who built the wall himself and then rode thru it. The boards were one inch and ran horizontal. About two years later he ran up a ramp, leaped over a water-sprinkling truck and the motor was completely wrecked, Ruggles escaping with a few minor cuts and bruises. Speed Ruggles is still riding, being at present a trick motorcyclist with the Victor McLaglen Motorcycle Corps. He has dropped the name of Speed and is now called Hap Ruggles. He also rides thru a 50-foot five-by-five-foot fire tunnel with both ends closed."*

"Fire Tunnel Crash"
Hap Ruggles

Member Edwin Phillips sez, "Hap was the guy who did the 'Fire Tunnel' because no one else wanted to do it."

WHEN the 29 members of the motorcycle unit of the Victor McLaglen Light Horse, Los Angeles, are not on parade or "pulling" hair-raising stunts they are performing less exciting tasks as employes of automotive parts stores, car dealerships and warehouses. "Happy" Ruggles, troop corporal and recording secretary, who is in the parts business, has sent MoToR a list of the group's feats which reads like a lot of Ripley believe-it-or-nots. One night a week after doing drills on motorcycles that the army does on foot they ride through plate glass, board walls, 17 feet of flaming burlap tunnel and then for good measure fall off their Harley-Davidsons and Indians while speeding 40 to 60 mph.

Those, says the corporal, are some of the dangerous stunts. Just ordinary tests of skill include 18 men riding on two cycles, four men standing on the shoulders of a driver speeding along with hands in the air, one man balanced on a driver's head, and such elemental tricks as riding backwards, spinning small circles, doing a trapeze act, with the cycles, on a pipe 14 feet high, and what have you.

The troop has paraded and performed at fairs, festivals, police shows, various other events and for the movies. This year they may go on a national tour. For nine weeks they traveled around California as worthy hosts for Mexico City's stunt policemen, called the "squadron of death." They have a club house and an illuminated stadium and track, and they have a lot of fun working out new ways of saving their necks while keeping fit as one of several units of the Light Horse commanded by Co. Victor McLaglen as a means of promoting friendships, Americanism and civic interests in case of emergency.

"The Swan"
Motorman: Hap Ruggles
Top: Jim Crawford
Rear Rack: Joe Stewart

"The Flying Trapeze"
Top-Center: Hap Ruggles
Left: Ernie Aguire
Right: Jimmy Crawford
Motorman: Wayne Fitzgerald

"The Flying Trapeze"
Top: Hap Ruggles
Motorman: Wayne Fitzgerald

In 1963, even though Hap wasn't riding with the team any longer, he attended a VMMC Old Timers' Picnic, held on September 8 and wrote an article which was published in several of the local Los Angeles newspapers. Approximately 130 current members including old timers, friends and family, and special guest, Mrs. McLaglen, were in attendance; Victor had passed away in 1959.

(L-R) Hap Ruggles, Unknown, Unknown, Unknown, Unknown, Howard Jester, Bing Bengston
In Front: Gracie Jester, Mrs. McLaglen 1963

The Motor Corps was indeed fortunate to have Hap along as a member. He was immensely valuable through those early years. What a guy!

Appendix M

Tom and Barbara Scott

The following article, "Raising the Bar & Shield," written by Laurie Watanabe, was printed in the Dealernews, Vol. 35, No. 1, January 1999. I thought it was very interesting as it describes the excellent business sense Tom Scott had in building a lucrative business in the motorcycling industry.

Working the parts counter are (from left) Brian Scott, Gene Crounk, Dallas Stone and Tom Scott.

Raising The Bar & Shield

Tom Scott, Harley-Davidson Of Fullerton's Owner, Has Spent His Life Championing The Sport He Loves

by Laurie Watanabe

Forty years ago, America was a simpler place. Back then, men were men, women were girls, and a double-cheeseburger with a chocolate malt was considered a well-rounded meal.

Tom Scott, owner of Harley-Davidson Of Fullerton in Fullerton, California, has his share of good memories from that era. After all, it was during that time that he fell in love — permanently — with Harley-Davidsons. "I'm the youngest of five, and my older brother had one," Tom, a Pennsylvania transplant, says. "I worked for my brother on the weekends and saved my money. I had my first Harley, bought and paid for, at 15. It was always Harley. I've never owned anything else." He laughs. "Brainwashed!"

However, he also contends that the motorcycling industry has come a long way since then — for the better, believe it or not.

"I'd never thought I'd see motorcycling evolve to what it is today," he says. "When I was growing up, if you rode a motorcycle, you were known as an uncouth, uneducated monster whose only interest was to make trouble for someone. I read that in the paper and wondered, even back then, how I could improve that image."

Raising The Stakes

In star-struck Southern California, where fame and fortune can be fast and fleeting, Harley-Davidson Of Fullerton's constancy is something of an anomaly. Just four miles from Disneyland, the landscape surrounding the dealership still included orange groves and family farms when the Scotts — Tom and his wife, Barbara — first moved to Fullerton in 1967. The family business was already two years old at that time, because the Scotts had originally opened a Harley dealership in 1966 in Santa Maria, a couple hundred miles north of Fullerton.

While Santa Maria is a picturesque place to visit, the Scotts found it difficult to build a successful store in a town known for oil wells and broccoli fields. Still, Tom — whose philosophy seems to be that even bad situations can be learned from — says he doesn't harbor ill will. "We learned the business there," he notes.

In a quirk of fate, a year later, the Scotts met a Harley dealer who was having troubles of his own. "He was tired of the rat race, and we were struggling in Santa Maria," Tom recalls. "We decided we either needed to go into a big city, where we could make a decent living, or walk away."

The solution: Swap stores. "We came down here in 1967, and he went up there," Tom says.

The Scotts settled into the Southern California store, which they named Harley-Davidson Of Fullerton. But they soon decided to build their own facility, and chose a location nearby with convenient freeway access. After purchasing the land, the Scotts built a one-story, 5,000 sq./ft. store in 1970, shortly after their son Brian was born (he's now the store's GM). "Other dealers asked, 'Are you crazy?' for spending that kind of money. It was a palace back then," Tom laughs.

In 1973, they expanded the service department. The physical layout of the facility stayed the same for the next decade or so, until Harley CEO Jeff Bleustein came to visit in 1984.

At a seminar given by store planner Clark Ritchie, Bleustein — at that time in the parts & accessories division — became enamored of a marketing concept called the "traffic loop," a way to clearly, if subconsciously, guide customers through the store. Bleustein's vision was to test the traffic loop on several existing Harley dealerships.

Tom listened intently. "T-shirts were just starting to come into the black," he says. "But we went through a period when we levelled off; we couldn't increase it anymore. So I told Clark, 'I'd like to sell more, but I don't know how. What can we do about this?' He said, 'Oh, you'd be surprised.'"

Soon after, Tom traveled to Oconomowac, Wisconsin, for Harley's national meeting. Bleustein and Ritchie were there, with a surprise. "They had my store all drawn out in picture form, with the traffic loop and everything!" Tom says.

He agreed to give the traffic loop a try, as did a store in New Hampshire and one in Harley's hometown of Milwaukee. Whatever trepidation Tom might have felt at the outset of the project was put to rest when he looked at his one-year sales figures. "We tracked it very, very carefully," he says. "In

A central skylight brightens the apparel departments for men (background) and women/children (foreground).

the first year of business with the traffic loop, our apparel sales doubled."

Tom was sold on the idea of working with his OEM and professional marketers to improve his business.

Raising The Roof

Fast forward to 1993. A decade has passed since the traffic loop revolutionized Harley-Davidson Of Fullerton's apparel business, and Tom was looking for something big for the rest of the store. In a word: expansion.

However, a lot had changed in the nearly 25 years since the Scotts first moved to Fullerton. Orange County was becoming known more for big business than dwindling orange groves. The Scotts and their "palace" were now surrounded by other properties. "We owned the property, and we still had great freeway access," Tom says, explaining why he didn't want to move. "I tried to buy that property" — he gestures to the building beyond his parking lot — "but the owner wouldn't sell to me."

The solution was obvious: If Harley-Davidson Of Fullerton couldn't expand outward, it would expand upward by adding a second story. Once again, Tom turned to design consultants and architects for their ideas and expertise. Once he had their input... he argued. Voraciously.

The plan was to build an extended showroom and parts & accessories department on the main floor, and to move apparel and collectibles, along with the customer lounge, upstairs. "But I didn't want to build a pair of staircases where people couldn't see what was up there," Tom says. He also wanted to prevent feelings of division between staff members. "There would be a gap," Tom says, "a feeling of 'Well, that person works upstairs.' I wanted to keep everyone together."

The answer was both simple and simply effective. Customers walking into the showroom today are immediately aware of two staircases on opposite sides, done in warm maple tones. The apparel on the second floor is clearly visible, thanks in part to large panes of frosted glass (expertly decorated with Harley etchings) instead of regular balustrades.

Raising The Bar & Shield

Glass balustrades give customers a peek at the apparel and collectibles upstairs, while making the Harley-Davidson Of Fullerton staff feel more like a cohesive group.

"Most people who come in see the stairs, so they know there's something up there," Tom says. "It makes them want to look up." A huge skylight in the cathedral-style roof brightens both floors; so does a giant neon Harley Bar & Shield with eagle on one wall. Opposite the eagle is a square, replaceable window visible from the street. Brian Scott, a serious stained glass hobbyist, is working on a Fatboy logo window for that spot. "It's one of the last little touches," Tom says.

The final result is a wide-open feeling, with both staff and merchandise clearly visible to customers and staff members who work on the first level. Tom admits this wasn't the least expensive way to add a second story, but adds, "We wanted our store to have a warm feeling. We wanted a modern approach, but a warm feel."

Technically, Harley-Davidson Of Fullerton is a tri-level store. The main staircases take customers to the men's apparel section on the second level; climb a few more stairs, and you'll find yourself on the store's third level, home to women's and children's apparel, collectibles and the ever-popular customer lounge. To the store's younger visitors, the lounge is like being at home... only better. Stocked with a Harley soda machine, vintage jukebox and pinball machine, in addition to the requisite sofa, table and chairs, the lounge also contains a coin-operated, pint-sized Harley, complete with headlights and *potato-potato-potato* sound effects.

While the new second story draws a lot of attention from regular customers, the first floor showroom and parts & accessories departments also benefitted from the expansion. The showroom grew, to give more room to the sales staff. Beyond the ➡

149

Raising The Bar & Shield

showroom, the parts & accessories crew is stationed at a long counter to help customers. Past the parts counter is a corridor leading outside to the service department. Determined to keep the store open during the renovation, the Scotts constructed a 2,600 sq./ft. building next to that service department to act as the temporary showroom and MotorClothes area while the store was being renovated.

"I thought we were going to be able to save the floor, but we had to put in a whole new one," Tom says. City ordinances even required a new parking lot, to make the service department wheelchair accessible. The Scotts *were* able to do some recycling: Beams that held a Harley-Davidson Of Fullerton marquis in a former life were reconditioned and are now incorporated into the "industrial-look" ceiling.

As challenging as it was to keep the store open during construction, Tom says being on the premises enabled Harley-Davidson Of Fullerton to complete their renovation in just six months. "If you're not in the store as it's being built, the builders can set their own pace. But we were there the whole time, asking, 'When is this going to go in? When are you going to get to that?'"

Raising The Standard

While a lot has changed at the renovated Harley-Davidson Of Fullerton, the store remains dedicated to the customer service that has made it successful for nearly 30 years.

"Customers today want variety," Tom notes. "They expect a lot out of specialized stores. Back when I was growing up, you had one jacket, and it *lasted*. Now, people don't have just two jackets, they have three or four. They like to have choices."

To cater to folks who are accustomed to shopping in malls and big-name department stores, Tom says, "Even mechanics need to have a certain amount of rapport with customers. Everyone has to be sales-minded. If you have a problem with your car, you go to a dealership, talk to a service writer and leave your car. That's the only contact you have with the dealership. But with a motorcycle, it's different. People who ride want to meet the mechanics who work on their bikes."

Over in the parts department, Tom says, "We do next-day ordering if we don't have something in stock. I get frustrated sometimes, because no matter how big an inventory you have, you can't have every single part in stock. Everybody wants everything to be turnkey." Then he smiles. "But I understand, too... we all want the same thing. We all want it *now*."

In the showroom, Tom adds, his reps do a good job of communicating with both long-time riders and the newer professional, white-collar enthusiasts. "We do an excellent job up front because we remember we're in the entertainment business," he says. "A guy on a motorcycle wants to forget his troubles. You can go to a movie, and the movie will last two hours, then it's over. But you can get on your motorcycle and make it last as long as you want. You can change into your leathers, change your personality, and off you go into another world. When you come back, you're ready to go to work."

Raising The Bar & Shield

Raising A Ruckus

Today, Harley-Davidson Of Fullerton seems the antithesis of the dark, dingy motorcycle shop stereotyped in Tom's youth. Tom admits he sometimes silently wondered, "How long is it going to take me to recoup these costs?" But in the end, he and his staff took the high-end road whenever possible. That meant hiring consultants and architects, then fighting to keep or create what the staff thought was important.

"I was talking with the builder, and he told me he had a little room for overflow inventory, but it was up on the top level. I told him, 'I've got to have a place to store the T-shirts, and I don't want them in view. There is no way we're running up there to get a T-shirt." The architect gave in and added a small, corridor-like space perfect for rows of T-shirts, right in the apparel department. Problem solved? Well...

"He put a big door on the room," Tom grins. "I said, 'I can't have this door here. This door is going to be opened more than 100 times a day and somebody's going to be walking by, and ... no!'" The final solution: Swinging, saloon-style doors that hide the inventory, but lend visibility for increased safety.

"The architect told me, 'I've done seven Harley stores, and I've never done that,'" Tom remembers. "I said, 'Well, you're doing it now.'

"Clark Ritchie and I argued about orange. He said, 'Orange doesn't match anything!' And I said, '*Orange*.'" The horizontal orange stripe around the new exterior of the store shows who won that round of negotiations. Placing the Bar & Shield on the corner of the building — where it's visible to traffic in two directions — was "ingenious," Tom says. The huge eagles on the windows were created by a mylar craftsman.

Tom hired other experts to do the woodwork that prominently sets the store's style, and matched the maple hues on the walls and stairs, another costly decision. He's almost sheepish as he opens the door to his second-floor office. Classical music plays over stereo speakers, his desk is maple and marble, and carpenters have just installed small spotlights in his personal collectibles cabinet next to the wet bar. A computer system sits on his desk; Brian created the store website, which does significant apparel sales and brings locals into the store for a closer look.

Does this look like the office of an uncouth, uneducated monster? Tom grins. "I spent a little money on it," he says, "after all those years of working out of a closet!" Then he becomes more thoughtful. "When it comes right down to it, it's just a building," he says. "I know everyone says this, but what makes the difference is how our staff makes customers feel."

And how the store's owner feels about the sport he's selling. "When I was 15, I used to wonder, 'When I'm 40, will I still want to ride?' I do. And it's just as enjoyable. Even more so."

Tom and Barbara in their Santa Maria Harley-Davidson store

Appendix N

Maria M Willers

The following pages are some of the humorous and informative accounts Maria experienced as the first female <u>ever</u> to become a drill-riding member of the No. 1, most fantastic motorcycle stunt and drill team in the country -- the Victor McLaglen Motor Corps (VMMC).

ThunderPress magazine, "The Maria Willers' Story, McLaglen's First Woman Joining the Corps." (Willers, M, May 2001).

The Maria Willers' Story

EVERYTHING YOU HAVE EVER WANTED TO KNOW ABOUT JOINING A MOTORCYCLE STUNT AND DRILL TEAM, BUT WERE AFRAID TO TRY

McLAGLEN'S FIRST WOMAN
Joining the Corps

by Maria Willers

Riding motorcycles has been a favorite pastime of mine for the last 10 years. Following a rather serious illness last year I was eager to get out on the road again. The opportunity of riding my red 1972 Shovelhead (which I named Scarlet Harlet) from Los Angeles, California to Yuma, Arizona for the annual Yuma Prison Run came up in April 2000, where I saw the famous Victor McLaglen Motor Corps perform. The announcer of the group mentioned there were four positions available in the group and any interested riders could approach them after the show for details. Although I wondered what it would be like to join such a group, thinking they would be "overwhelmed" with prospective members, I decided not to seek them out. There was one other problem I didn't mention … I'm a woman and this is an all male group.

Upon my return home, I happened to mention the group to some friends and asked if the stunt and drill team had ever entertained the idea of a female member. One of my friends said, "Why don't you ask Harry?" Harry is the colonel of the Victor McLaglen group and he lived in Bellflower, California which was right down the street from my home. Before there was time to change my mind, Harry Fisher had interviewed me and, subsequently, introduced me to the team at the next meeting. Everyone seemed very supportive and the group had a way of making you feel "part of" it.

I'd like to end the story here and say that I performed beautifully and fit right into the group without any difficulty. Unfortunately, that wasn't the case because I had to learn how to ride all over again. The sense that people were watching me during this process was not far fetched, because I was the first woman ever to try for admittance into the team. I realized very quickly that if I didn't get up to speed in a relatively short period of time, people might say a woman had no place in this group because we physically could not do it.

Most of the drill maneuvers are done at a very low rate of speed, not exceeding 12 mph. This slow speed and the expertise shown in maneuvering these motorcycles is what makes the team stand out from the ordinary rider. Mark Frymoyer, one of the riders in the group who does a lot of the solo stunts, stopped by a couple of days after my first meeting and took my motorcycle out for a spin. Before I could gasp, he was standing on Scarlet's seat as the motorcycle traveled down the street. He also let the bike pivot around him while he held her left handlebar. He kept his right foot on the floorboard and he performed a tight circle. When he brought the motorcycle back to me, he said, "Well, at least we know one thing now….the bike can do it!"

Since the owner of the motorcycle needed all the help she could get, Mark suggested learning slow tight circles in order to develop balance. This maneuver is done by moving at a very slow speed, rotating in a tight circle, slipping the clutch, braking, and, most importantly, keeping your feet up on the floorboards. If you are very good, you are not holding the handlebars at all -- total balance. Since turning corners was not my favorite thing, I immediately started practicing. My large circles slowly got tighter and tighter. About a week into this valiant attempt to defy gravity, during a telephone conversation with Ruth, Harry's wife, I talked about my attempts to learn this maneuver. Ruth started laughing and informed me that doing a slow tight circle was not required for membership. However, she suggested that in my case, it might be wise to learn something like the tight circle so people would not challenge my right to be a team member.

Maria Greets a Fan

Love Ride - Castaic, California
Left: Maria Willers

The Colonel, his son Marty, and Mark worked with me to further develop my skills. To watch them ride in front of me was so disheartening. Mark and Marty just flowed over the asphalt. They made riding an 800-pound motorcycle look like ballet. Totally discouraged at one point, I stopped dead in my tracks. Sensing my discomfort and dismay, Harry wisely allowed me to follow Mark who was riding to the left. "Swooping" around the riding course like one of the team members felt great.

In the dumps - Thrills were frequently followed by despair. Mark, trying to be helpful and very honest, said I rode like I was pointing my motorcycle in the general direction I wanted it to go and hoped it would get there. All these years of riding, and some stranger was telling me how to get where I was going. He was right, though. Team members were able to smartly turn their motorcycles either to the right or the left, and did this without any appearance of hesitation or unsteadiness. Back to the drawing board for me. Counter-steering was the next subject. If you want to go left, you have to point your motorcycle to the right. This shifts your weight and allows you to dip to the left. You can also turn to the left or the right by pulling in your clutch and turning your bike in the direction you intend to go. As your bike starts to fall, you let out your clutch and the momentum pulls you up. Or, you can turn around with momentum that

Motorcycle Safety Foundation (MSF) doesn't teach this maneuver

carries you through the intended action. And, let's not forget the use of your legs and body to make this motorcycle change directions. Riding "like a lady," legs together and sitting up straight, was actually hindering my progress. Soon, Mark had me throwing my left or right knee out hard as I flew into a tight turn while shifting my upper body in the opposite direction of the turn. Sometimes I got so confused about what body part went in what direction that I couldn't do anything but come to a stop in total hysterics from laughter.

Scarlet Harlet, my beautiful Roman Red 1972 Harley-Davidson FL Shovelhead, slowly began to change. Down went her handlebars, off came her windshield and side mirrors, and up came her hand controls. A heel clutch was installed on the left side to allow my hands to be free to hang on to other team members during certain drills. In order to give my motorcycle a little more stability, flat profile tires were installed. The highway pegs were removed and bumpers were placed on all four crash bars – automobile water hoses, cut down the middle and wrapped with electrical tape. Then, if the motorcycle went down, she would just rock on the bars without any damage to the chrome. If I ever gained approval for membership, Scarlet's paint job would have to be changed to black and white, similar to a police motorcycle. Scarlet had been my beautiful red lady for many years, so it was difficult to picture her in any other color.

I practiced out on a dead-end street for the first three weeks until politely asked to leave. The complaint of noise was as a valid one, so I went in search of a vacant lot. Finding one, Mark immediately decided the painted parking lanes could be used to teach me how to go very slowly down a straight line. Once again, I was back in kindergarten trying to hold that 800-pound bike still enough to slowly go down a straight line. Every try resulted in the bike falling to the left or the right, and down my feet would go. Mark kept telling me to pick up my feet, and said that no matter what happened, my feet were not to touch the ground. Of course, I made excuses for my poor riding by telling Mark that the change in location was affecting me. In return, Mark mimicked me by saying, "Harry, I can't ride in this parade because I'm more comfortable in that parade." Enough said. Mark had made his point. Riding with the group would happen on asphalt, dirt and grass, in sunshine or in rain, and all riders were expected to do well, no matter what environment we faced.

Fascinated by a team maneuver I observed at a recent show, I tried to copy it. The lead motorcycle pulls to a stop and the other team members ride their motorcycle one by one up to the right of the stopped motorcycle. Without putting their feet down, they step on the heel clutch, brake the bike, and grab the right shoulder of the team member immediately to their left. When the formation is ready to move, each member again, one by one, releases the brake, opens the clutch slowly, and without putting their feet down, moves away. Do you remember the Western movie years ago where a drunken cowboy and his horse were leaning against a building? Yep, that was me trying this stunt. I would get within two to three feet of a lamppost, would pull my heal clutch in and tighten my brake, and would try to grab the lamp post with my left hand. It's like rubbing your stomach with your right hand while patting your head with your left hand, and doing the two-step with your feet while you balance 800 pounds of solid steel.

Cone removal - At the first practice, with my jumpsuit on, I waited (scared to death) for the firing squadron. The only way to learn was to jump in with both feet and I was ready as much as was possible. With whistles blowing, we started off by following a set routine of getting on the motorcycles, then going through cones separated 12 feet apart – not the 15 feet I had been practicing. I kept missing the cones or riding over them, which required someone to come out and remove them from the bottom of my bike.

Not having any clue what the precision drill routine was, I blindly followed the leader. In spite of the difficulty, there were some brilliant moments on my part, however fleeting they were. At one point, a rider accidentally came up on my left side.

This required me to remove my left hand from the clutch and use my heel clutch clutch while I reached over and took hold of his shoulder. Wrong move! Not being familiar with the heel clutch, I almost ran into a building. The team kept on going and we did a few more maneuvers which paired me up with a different rider. As we went around in a circle -- while leaning into the other rider -- down I went. Scarlet and I hit the ground with her throttle side open. Instead of shutting off the engine, I frantically tried to grab her throttle – wrong move again. Scarlet's mirror was shattered, the spotlights were loose, and I was mortified. The team stopped, picked Scarlet up, dusted us off, and then we all finished the drill. I knew in my heart that getting right back up on the bike and finishing practice was imperative to gaining the team members' respect. We stopped for a short time to catch our breath, then did it all over again. I was so hyped up from the first drill that I got off the bike without thinking and forgot to put the kickstand down. Down Scarlet went again. I was really making points. We finished the second practice and Mark came over to let me know how entertaining my performance had been.

During the next two weeks, I continued to practice daily. At the second practice, Mark led the drills. He stopped the group several times until he had Sam situated where he would be my partner. Sam is a very strong, steady rider -- just right for me. This time, I did fairly well and only messed up once, turning in front of an oncoming rider.

When we stopped, several of the riders thought I should start trying some stunts. Before I could protest, I was hanging sideways off of Sam's bike. He looked as surprised as me, because he had never done the Half P-38 stunt himself. They taught me how to get on and off a moving motorcycle, how to grab the handlebar and, finally, how to keep my center of gravity in the middle. Taking my instructions seriously, I got Sam in a neck hold that actually blocked his vision while we traveled around the parking lot. Sam and I were laughing, and the group was threatening to call his wife. Following that practice, my neighbors frequently caught me hanging sideways off the end of my truck's tailgate, trying to develop strength and get the feel of hanging there. I'm sure they thought I had finally lost my marbles.

The third practice was the first one with Harry Fisher, the Colonel. Now that was a practice. We were out there working on precision drills and stunts for almost three hours. It was so hot, I lost four pounds. To make matters worse, Scarlet's shifter peg had fallen off on the way to practice and her transmission was acting up. Then, Harry decided to do the maneuver I had been training for when trying to pull up to a lamppost. I was so nervous. If I lost my balance and fell, the entire row of riders might possibly go down with me.

Amazingly, I was able to pull up to Mighty Moe, grab his shoulder and use my heel clutch without putting my feet on the ground, but we were very close. All Moe had to do was turn his right foot out and he could have placed it on Scarlet's floorboard...very chummy I'd say.

After we had done the precision drill, Harry decided it was time to practice stunts. He informed me that I was to do the Half P-38 stunt with him, not Sam. Although I politely informed him that I had never actually done the stunt, his response was, "Well, today you're going to do it." Putting my fear aside, I mounted Harry's motorcycle in preparation for the stunt. Harry again instructed me to keep my center of gravity in towards the middle of the bike to prevent him from losing his balance. When he gave me the signal, I prepared for the stunt and then went down the side of the motorcycle. I wasn't afraid initially because Harry is an extremely strong rider, but when he started going in circles during the stunt, that scared me since it was such an odd feeling to see everything circling you sideways.

Come back here - Surviving that stunt, I thought I was done for the day. Wrong again ... when am I going to learn? Now, Harry wanted me to try and stand up on a rider's shoulders. Poor Big Mike and Sam, I was afraid of hurting their shoulders. I had to get up on their motorcycles from the back and then climb up on their shoulders in one move, using Sam's helmet to boost me up. This turned out to be a problem. After finally reaching my goal, Mark showed me how to use the rope to steady myself, and how to stand and wave to the crowd. Next, Harry suggested doing a handstand. Me, a woman, doing a handstand? Right! The handstand required me to get up on the back of two bikes, straddling them, with my hands on the shoulders of the riders. When they gave me the signal, I was supposed to pick up my feet and place my legs on the shoulders of Moe standing behind me. Then, I was to push up with my arms while Moe held up my legs. I had a dickens of a time. Before Mighty Moe could get my legs up where they belonged, I closed them right around his neck. That sent everyone into stitches. Moe and I were really getting to know each other that day.

Lost cause? My fourth practice with the group came all too soon and this one had an agility test to boot. The "S" curve, paced out with cones, was about 4-feet wide and had a sharp turn to the right and then the left. I watched some of the riders try to go through it. Cones were being knocked down all over the place. Thinking I should give it a whirl, I started into the right turn. Try as I might, I couldn't even get through the first turn. If I had to pass this agility test to win membership, it was a lost cause.

Harry started the practice and put the team through the cones several times. I didn't get through the course once. I usually ended up riding out the side of the "S" curve after the first turn because I couldn't turn to the right tightly enough. Then, the team went over to the larger parking lot and went through their paces. We started with the stunt where we hang onto each other without putting our feet down. We did it twice and both times Scarlet died–not a good sign. Harry then announced to the group that it was my fourth practice and it was time to vote on my membership. He said a few words regarding his past feelings about having a woman on the team, spoke briefly about his initial interview with me, then asked me to say a few words. Taken by surprise, I told the members I had always admired them and was happy to have had an opportunity to meet and work with them. I was asked to step away from the group while they voted, and was told I would receive a letter in the mail regarding the decision.

I stood over on the side having a soda while everyone voted on little yellow slips of paper. Harry finally called me back, saying he didn't want to waste any postage. He handed me a yellow slip of paper and said, "You're in." I couldn't believe my ears. I had done it. They voted to have me as a new member. Unbelievable. I started jumping up and down, hugged Harry, and then hugged Mark. One of the members later came up to me and let me know the vote was unanimous and not one person had anything bad to say about me. You have to understand how that just blew me away. I was so honored and yet so humbled because these men had faith in me.

The next year is going to be exciting to say the least. I now have the challenge of pushing myself to develop skills above and beyond anything I ever felt I might be capable of achieving, but this will take time. Part of the thrill of reaching this goal will be performing with all the members of the Victor McLaglen club. My father had a saying that "YOU can accomplish ANYTHING if you set your mind to it." I have decided to become one of the better riders this club has had and being a girl will not be an excuse to do poorly. Time and LOTS of practice will be major factors in whether this goal is reached. Until my next update a year from now, "Keep the rubber on the road."

Postscript - This is a story of meeting challenges, gaining acceptance and, ultimately, achieving the high honor of being the first woman to perform with the world-famous Victor McLaglen Motor Corps. It is told by the amazing woman who lived it, Maria Willers, but it doesn't end here. Maria has now ridden with the group for a solid year, and recently traveled with them on the International Motorcycle Show Tour, performing in Minneapolis, Cleveland, Chicago and St. Louis (doing nine shows each weekend). Maria reports that it was quite an experience and she didn't fall down once. The guys continue to torment her with practical jokes, like hiding Scarlet (her bike), or applying bullet hole appliques all over it and saying they shot at a bike thief and missed. She gets back at them in her own subtle way, which can involve their riding boots and something with potato chips; not to incriminate her in any way. And, you know the old adage: They wouldn't tease her if they didn't like her. Maria's newest payback of all, though, is the faint pink pinstripe decorating the otherwise Victor McLaglen regulation paint job on her beloved bike. She insists that Colonel Harry Fisher has never noticed, but it may just be because he can't help but like her.

(R-L) Tedd Farrell, Bruce Chubbuck, Mark Frymoyer & Maria line up with the team

"Speedo"
Maria & Mark
Honda's "Ride for Kids" 2001

In 2003, Maria relocated Nevada. This letter from Harry Fisher, VMMC Drill Leader, was the Corps' official response to Maria's request for resignation. The tone and contents of the letter speaks to Maria's value to the team.

"WORLD CHAMPION" MOTORCYCLE STUNT AND DRILL TEAM

February 16, 2003

Ms. Maria Willers
P.O. Box 783
Caliente, NV. 89008

Dear Maria:

Your letter arrived this week and we were disappointed that you would no longer be riding with the team. Your membership in this unique organization was a definite boost in endearing us to women riders. Your article on what it's like to be a new member, gave us a little more exposure, your friend Sam Jones was a big help in shooting a new set of photos for us to work with, and through your particpation in the team, we were able to sign up Sue as a new member. We do appreciate these things and do thank you for putting in the extra effort involved in helping.

I think all in all, you'll agree, your skills improved immensely during the past two years and that's a good thing that will stay with you for the rest of your life. I doubt that you will have a need to do a "Speedo" or drive a "Front Fender Layback", but you undoubtedly will have a need to turn a tight U-turn and ride slowly through bad road conditions.

Again, we are sorry you can no longer be an active member of this team, but we certainly understand your predicament. To leave in good standing with the team, we will need to have your uniform shirts, britches, helmet, and any other Motor Corps equipment you might have, returned in good condition. You can bring this to any one of our members on your next trip to L.A., if you'd like. Once they are returned, we will send your full 2003 dues refund of $20 to you.

Good luck to you in your retirement in Caliente.

Sincerely,

Harry

Harry Fisher
Drill Leader

Appendix O

World War II (WWII)
How It Affected The Victor McLaglen Motor Corps

Every war affects the population; not only the soldiers, but also their families, friends and society as a whole. World War II wasn't any different. It definitely had an influence on the Victor McLaglen Motor Corps (VMMC) and its members.

The articles in this section were written by our members during World War II. These writings serve as indicators of the mood shared by countless Americans, as well as the role our Motor Corps played on the world stage. I don't know the origin or where some of these publications originated, because numerous articles came from newspapers or magazines and were cut and pasted in a scrapbook. Many of those articles were printed in local California newspapers such as *The Los Angeles Examiner*, *Los Angeles Press Herald*, *Los Angeles Times*, *Long Beach Press Telegram*; and national publications including *The Motorcyclist* magazine, *The Enthusiasts*, etc. Motor Corps member, Hap Ruggles, often served as the team reporter and publicist, and contributed pieces to most of these publications.

I know the membership declined in numbers during WWII due to so many of the men being sent to war, but to hear the angst and patriotism in their scripts made it feel even more real to me. By 1945, the 35-member-strong VMMC count had dwindled to about seven, the war ended and by 1949, the team had reorganized and the membership had grown to 33 members. They were back in full swing -- performing and traveling the countryside.

I've included some of the teams' writings. As indicated earlier, I was not always able to find information regarding where and when some of these pieces were published. They were stored in boxes of Motor Corps pictures and articles, and were often cut or torn from newspapers, magazines, periodicals, meeting minutes or notices, etc. Perhaps, some of them were never even published. They do, however, demonstrate the feelings and situations experienced by many of our members during the war years.

Victor McLaglen Motor Corps World War II Timeline

1935   Motor Corps consisted of 17 Charter members

1938   Membership increased to 35 members

1941   Pearl Harbor attacks on December 7th
- United States enters WWII
- Total of 20 Motor Corps members are serving in the military
- Thirteen of remaining 20 members are working in defense jobs – shipyards, aircraft industry, etc.
- All Corps members – not in the military service – received first aid cards and completed first aid, bomb, fire and evacuation classes (offered through civilian defense and police departments)

1945   WWII Ends – May 8th
- Per Hubie Phillips, seven members remain in the Motor Corps
- Five of seven members included Nick DeRush, Dale McCullum, Hubie Phillips, Hap Ruggles, Jim Underwood (others not listed)

1948   February - Motor Corps membership climbed from seven to 28 members

1949   January - Motor Corps membership was 33
               Two original members remained - Nick and Hap

Victor McLaglen Motor Corps Members

1. DeRush, Nick
2. Ruggles, Hap
3. Allen, Sidney
4. Allum, William
5. Behling, Harvey
6. Bengston, Edward
7. Benton, Lawrence
8. Bettleman, Harold
9. Bignell, Don
10. Blaesser, Frank
11. Block, Don
10. Butler, Rolls
11. Costa, Leo
12. Cromer, Pete
13. Dyerly, Elmo
14. Eastin, Sterling
15. Ervin, Virgil
16. Fenton, James
19. Greenwood, John
20. Griggs, Charles
21. Erickson, Phil
22. Hasselbring, Bob
19. Haynes, Lorin
20. Kemp, Stanley
21. Lewis, William
22. Locke, Otto
23. Palomarez, Fernando
28. Parsons, James
29. Phillips, Edwin
30. Phillips, Ray
31. Rayzor, Ken
32. Tegland, LeVern
33. Widdup, Vern

Harley-Davidson Races to the Defense of our Soldiers

Following the Japanese bombing of Pearl Harbor on December 7th, the United States declared war on Japan. Three days later, after Germany and Italy declared war, the United States became fully engaged in the Second World War.

This meant, of course, that those members of the VMMC, who responded to our nation's call of duty, were ready to show the enemy a thing or two.

It is interesting to note Harley-Davidson was the main supplier of motorcycles to the United States military during World War II. The U.S. Armed Forces and their allies (including Great Britain, Canada and Russia) received in excess of 88,000 WLA models produced by Harley-Davidson.

By 1940, the production of the WLA occurred in relatively small numbers as a part of the military expansion plan that was being felt throughout the United States.
There was, however, a significant increase in production as the war continued. In fact, over 90,000 were produced (including spare parts) during WWII.

Harley-Davidson WLA

Blackout tail lamp as a combat zone imperative

Pictures from The Auto Editors of Consumer Guide "1942 Harley-Davidson WLA and XA" 13 September 2007. HowStuffWorks.com. <https://auto.howstuffworks.com/1942-harley-davidson-wla-and-xa.htm> 24 July 2022

Although the number of WLA's produced after WWII decreased, their quantities escalated again during the Korean War (1949-1952).

Chronological Events Leading to US Involvement in WWII (1941)

13 JAN	All persons born in Puerto Rico are declared US citizens by birth
20 JAN	President Franklin Roosevelt (FDR) begins his 3rd presidential term
23 JAN	Aviator Charles Lindbergh testifies before the US Congress to recommend USA negotiate a neutrality pact with Adolf Hitler
09 FEB	Winston Churchill requests USA show support by sending arms to the British . . . "*Give us the tools, and we will finish the job*"
11 MAR	President Roosevelt signs Lend-Lease into law, providing for US to Provide military equipment to Allies
27 MAR	Japanese spy, Takeo Yoshikawa, arrives in Honolulu, Hawaii and begins studying US fleet at Pearl Harbor
30 MAR	All German, Italian and Danish ships anchored in US waters taken into "protective custody"
10 APR	USN destroyer, *Niblack,* drops depth charges on German U-boat (first "shot in anger" fired by America against Germany)
25 APR	Lindbergh resigns commission in US Army Air Corps Reserve following criticism from FDR
01 MAY	First Series E "War Bonds" and Defense Savings Stamps go on sale
14 JUN	All German and Italian assets in the US are frozen
16 JUN	All German and Italian consulates in US are ordered closed and staffs ordered to leave country by July 10
20 JUN	US Army Air Forces replaces former US Army Air Corps.
26 JUL	• In response to Japanese occupation of French Indochina, FDR orders seizure of all Japanese assets in the US • General Douglas MacArthur named commander of all US forces in the Philippines; the Philippine Army is ordered nationalized
30 JUL	US gunboat *Tutuila* is attacked by Japanese aircraft while anchored in the Yangtze River at Chungking; Japan apologizes the next day

01 AUG	FDR bans export of US aviation fuel from western hemisphere except to Britain and allies.
09 AUG	FDR and Winston Churchill meet and Atlantic Charter is created
12 AUG	US House of Representatives passes (by one vote) legislation extending draft period from one year to 30 months
04 SEP	- USS *Greer* becomes the first US naval ship fired upon by a German submarine in the war (even though US is a neutral power) - Tension heightens between the nations
11 SEP	- Lindbergh accuses British, Jews and the Roosevelt administration of leading the US to war - Widespread condemnation of Lindbergh follows
17 OCT	Destroyer USS *Kearny* torpedoed by German submarine *U-568* off Iceland, killing 11 sailors (1st American military casualties of WWII)
10 NOV	Winston Churchill makes a speech in London stating, *should the United States become involved in war with Japan, the British will follow within the hour."*
17 NOV	Joseph Grew, US Ambassador to Japan, cables a warning to Washington, D.C. declaring Japan may strike suddenly and unexpectedly at any time
27 NOV	All US military forces in Asia and the Pacific are placed on war alert
01 DEC	Fiorello La Guardia, Mayor of New York City and Director of the Office of Civilian Defense, signs Administrative Order 9, creating Civil Air Patrol under authority of the US Army Air Forces
06 DEC	FDR make a personal peace appeal to Emperor Hirohito of Japan
07 DEC	**Attack on Pearl Harbor** Imperial Japanese Navy Air Services stages a military strike on US Navy at Pearl Harbor in Hawaii
08 DEC	- 12:30 (EST) – President Franklin D. Roosevelt gives his Infamy Speech to Joint Session of Congress - United States declaration of war on Japan is signed (within the hour)

1941 and World War *II* were heating up… as were the McLaglens

We have two new members, Vandermeulen and Blaesser, and have three applications on hand. In these times. We do not have much to offer for excitement, but if those slant-eyed &%$* come over we will have enough rubber as a whole to run quite a few months yet.

Our open house which we hold once or twice a year will be held in July this year with Jim Underwood and Vic Bell the chairmen. In addition to the men we have in the services, thirteen of the remaining twenty members are working on defense jobs, with two or three more leaving soon for the shipyards. As far as the club goes we are doing our bit in this world conflict.

For the first time in seven years we are not in the annual police show. The cause this year is that it is to be held in the shrine auditorium on the stage, which is too small to handle our motors. We will probably be called out to help with the traffic, as it is for four days instead of one.

We are starting soon with the plan of having our dues paid to the club in defense stamps. They are to be recorded and put away each month and are the property of the club.

We in California are fortunate so far regarding the gasoline rationing, Oregon and Washington are already rationed. Perhaps in the future we will be in the same boat in order to save rubber and repairs.

In this time and place we all have to sacrifice many things which if mentioned a year ago we would have brought a laugh, in a country where you can say what you want to and do what you want to at any time. Since the "chips are down" the Victor McLaglen Motor Corps is ready for any job that will help this great country of ours to remain free. And, as we paid our taxes we are now going to smash the axis…damn them.

*- **Hap Ruggles***

The Enthusiast Magazine
January 1942, Page 16

VICTOR McLAGLEN MCY. CORPS, Los Angeles, Calif. --- This year has nearly gone and it has been one of the busiest in the history of the Motor Corps. We traveled close to 600,000 motorcycle miles, and as Santa Claus will be pulling into town now pretty soon, we are busy preparing for the Tournament of Roses Parade. November was a busy month for us with parades. Besides having two shows for the month, we also led the Christmas Parade downtown in Los Angeles and also the mammoth Festival of Bands in Long Beach where 67 various musical organizations paraded. This parade is held annually and was witnessed by 350,000.

At our last open house we went roller skating and most of the members were down more than they were up. Our next open house we are going to Earl Carroll's for a party. We are now preparing a big Christmas get-together with the proceeds to be used for Christmas baskets for the needy. We hope to give about 18 baskets this year if our plans pan out. It is our great moment presenting those baskets to the needy and take it from us it is not a happy job especially where there are children in the home. We have four new members, Fenton, Burry, Raizer and Riley and we welcome them into our fold. This brings the membership up to 29 men even if Uncle Sam did take 8 of our members. Three of them are now motorcycle instructors. Plans are going ahead to remodel our club house and grounds in the near future with the building of a foreign city within our grounds and the plans call for the changing of the foreign city or village about four times a year. This will not affect our drill field. It is a great and unique idea and should be very interesting to all those who come to our grounds.

- Hap Ruggles

The Enthusiast Magazine
October 1942

McLAGLEN MOTORYCLE CORPS, Hollywood, Cal. – Well, lads and lassies of the motorcycle world, here we are for the first time in quite a spell as we have been very busy out here on the coast getting things in shape for a reception of Tojo, Hitler and Mussolini Inc. in case they should be foolish enough to come. We put on two shows the past month for two nearby Army Camps along with the USO that was studded with big name talent from the studio and entertainment world. After our performance, the Commanding Officer wanted to sign all of us up for his company saying that Tokio (sic) wouldn't have a chance with us. The boys really ate up our little offering of entertainment.

We had the pleasure of having two well known men stop off in Los Angeles and pay our club a visit. None other than Wm. H. Davidson and Wm. J. Harley. They had arrived here that morning from Shangri-la where they had been watching their iron horses go through their paces on a sand course. They then gave very interesting talks. It was certainly a pleasure meeting them and being able to show them around.

On the ninth of September we had our open house party and this time it was for all members, past and present. It was held at the Riviera on the outskirts of Chinatown and was attended by 67 persons some of whom we had not seen in years. It was a regular old fashioned get-together down at the country store. Of course, they had that long piece of furniture there where we partook of soft drinks and such, mostly such. We had a choice of southern fried chicken or top sirloin steak dinner. The committee of Underwood and Phillips did an excellent job of arranging the dinner and the items that go with a swell evening. The guests that we had for the evening were Mr. & Mrs. Chet Billings of the A.M.A. and editor of the Motorcyclist magazine, along with Lieut. Joe Gaalken and his wife. The Lieutenant is from the Sheriff's Office here in the city and has charge of the main control room in a secret building. They both gave very interesting talks on their work and the duties we will all have to do in times of emergency as we have all finished our first aid, bomb, fire and excavation classes. It looks now as though we are going to lose three or four more members to the service and when they go that will make 18 men in the armed forces. Where they all are now we do not know, but wherever you are, soldiers, we want you to know we wish you well and that you are giving them hell. To all you boys who have left your old saddle buddies and have new ones now in the service we wish you "happy riding" and God bless you.

                                                            - Hap Ruggles

In the 1950s and 1960s, prospective Motor Corps members were given an application which would be approved or disapproved by the membership. The application included this statement "Would you, in time of necessity, be willing to serve in a voluntary capacity, in Civil Defense, for as long as you are needed, without thought of remuneration?" Before acceptance into the Motor Corps, the applicant was obliged to sign, thus agreeing to this requirement.

Below is a sample application from that period. I could not find applications for the period 1935 through 1940, nor a statement of this Civil Service duty requirement. It appears this was a request made during or in the aftermath of WWII.

```
APPLICATION FOR MEMBERSHIP

NAME _____
ADDRESS _____
HOME PHONE _____
PHONE AT WORK _____
EMPLOYED BY _____
ADDRESS _____
YOUR A. M. A. NO. _____
DRIVERS'S LIC. NO. _____

Would you, in time of necessity, be willing
to serve in a voluntary capacity, in Civil
Defense, for as long as you are needed,
without thought of remuneration? _____

              SIGNED _____

              DO NOT WRITE BELOW.

REMARKS:



SPONSORED BY: _____
```

The following page was received by the Motor Corps from the Harley-Davidson Motor Company for their services.

We are proud of you motorcycle riders in Civilian Defense

EVERY motorcycle rider in Civilian Defense is a modern Paul Revere—instantly ready in any emergency to serve home and country. With no thought of remuneration or acclaim, he and his speedy, trusty mount await only duty's call. Patriotic citizens, familiar with his work and his sacrifice, are proud of him. As long as America can boast of such men, no foe from within or without can batter down the ramparts of freedom.

From all over the country come reports of the splendid work motorcycle clubs, enrolled in Civilian Defense, are already doing. In many cities, police forces are unequal to the task of convoying army contingents. Time and again, motorcyclists are coming to the rescue and our armed forces move to destination without delay and loss of precious time. When sirens screech and blackouts ensue, motorcyclists patrol and see that all rules and regulations are rigorously enforced.

In hundreds of communities, members of motorcycle clubs are taking first aid training, learning about fighting fire and gas, drilling for police duty—all to make themselves more efficient should the emergency arise. If lines of communication should fail, motorcycle riders will carry the messages to destination—if roads and highways are impassable to other vehicles, they will get through.

If your club has not yet affiliated with your local Civilian Defense effort, you should give the matter consideration at your very next meeting. Write the American Motorcycle Association, 8 East Long Street, Columbus, Ohio, for full instructions. The need is great and in this hour of the Nation's peril every motorcyclist is ready and anxious to do his full part in the protection and defense of the country we love so well—"the land of the free and the home of the brave."

Harley-Davidson Motor Company
Milwaukee, Wisconsin, U.S.A.

Even the local Harley shop had to stop business during the war, as noted by the letter below from Harley-Davidson in Hollywood, Inc.

By the way, Harry Sorenson who's name is at the bottom, was Harry Fisher's Uncle Harry. He was a Harley-Davidson certified mechanic.

DEAR CUSTOMER:

For twelve years we have been rendering Harley-Davidson Service in Hollywood. During that time, we have built up a large business and many grand friendships.

Due to the National Defense Program, we have been unable to get any new 1942 motorcycles for civilian use at all, and we have also suffered considerably for the lack of new parts. Now that the United States is 100% in this war, we have been notified that the parts situation will be even more serious. It is certain that each and every one of us will feel the restrictions of the use of steel, aluminum, copper and rubber, in one way or another, but war calls for sacrifices at home as well as at the front, so LET'S ALL DO OUR PART.

We have therefore decided to close our store and combine it with the main Harley-Davidson Agency, which is owned and operated by Rich Budelier, at 2531 South Main Street, Los Angeles.

We expect to close August 15th, 1942.

All the books and accounts will be turned over to the following address. You are asked to pay all bills and payments on motorcycles due us, at 2531 South Main Street, where you will receive your receipts. We shall later on be working at the main Harley-Davidson Agency, and shall be glad to meet and greet all our old friends.

Our factory is running at top speed making thousands and thousands of motorcycles and parts for the Armed Forces--motorcycles that will be used to help beat Hitler, Mussolini and Hirohito.

We dislike closing our store and being unable to render the convenient service you like, as much as our factory dislikes not being able to furnish us with motorcycles and parts so we can render you that service.

However, after we have "WON THE WAR" we will "WIN THE PEACE," and when PEACE has come to this War-torn World again, we shall again open up in Hollywood in a BIGGER AND BETTER WAY than ever before. Something that will meet your dream and ours, in a model MOTORCYCLE STORE.

Yours truly,

BEN WEBB, Manager   Geo. Straehle

Phil Steyer   Harry Sorensen

Hubie Phillips
The Enthusiast Magazine
January 1945

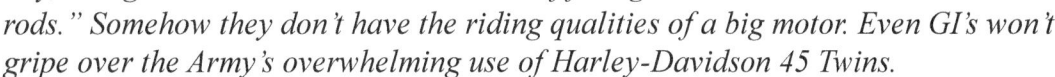

From a McLaglen Motor Corp Member in England
The latest copy of our magazine was very welcome in my mail the other day. At least us boys in the service can read about cycles even if we don't get a chance to ride. My wife tells me that my riding fund at home will now cover a new 7 OHV job. Boy, let's get this war won! I've seen a lot of foreign "hot rods." Somehow they don't have the riding qualities of a big motor. Even GI's won't gripe over the Army's overwhelming use of Harley-Davidson 45 Twins.

The McLaglen club has almost ceased to exist as far as activities are concerned. What with only seven members left in the organization to carry on. And in addition. they are doubling up on most of their work. That doesn't leave much material and time in which to meet and observe club regulations. But with the ending of this war you will find us kicking around again getting in everyone's hair including Rich Budelier's and behaving like the gang of old. Hap Ruggles has a job on his hands keeping his Los Angeles Motor Escort business going with the shortage of riders. Understand that Nick DeRush was machining at night and riding for Hap days. Jim Underwood I hear is making the P-61 out there and our old friend Dale McCullum rides herd on the convoys for Lockheed. Ray Phillips (no kin but a darn good guy) has bounced out of uniform. He's able to ride a motorcycle as usual, but is classified as over-age for military service. Joel Stewart is out there doing his part in the war effort but just what I don't know. The rest of the boys are all over the world by now cussing no doubt because they haven't anything faster to chase the Axis with than two good feet like me. Keep making those good motorcycles and we boys will keep them rolling, now and later.

Cpl. Hubert J. Phillips

Corporal Hubie

Appendix P

Articles and Pictures from Motorcycle Publications – 1939-1949

During the early years of the Motor Corps, there were many publications that depicted their activities in write-ups and pictures. Many of these were written and submitted by charter member Hap Ruggles and published in *The Enthusiast* motorcycle magazine. I thought they might be of interest and are reproduced here for your perusal.

December 1939
Page 15

Presenting the famous Victor McLaglen Motorcycle Corp., Los Angeles, California

In front are: Sergeant McCollum, left, Lieutenant Crawford, Lieutenant Colonel Mrs. Hal Roach, Captain DeRush, Lieutenant Ruggles and Sergeant Phillips.

The Enthusiast Magazine
January 1940
Page 18

VICTOR McLAGLEN MCY. CORPS, Los Angeles, Calif. – As vacation time is all over, all the boys are back and in the saddle, working hard for the coming events. Secretary Hap Ruggles visited his home town, Portland, Oregon, recently and was treated royally by the members of the Rose City Motorcycle Club, and also by the Harley-Davidson dealer, Mr. Geo. W. Schantin, and his right-hand man, Mr. Fred Marshall.

On the 19th of November we put on a show for the Actors Guild of Hollywood. A week later, we put on a show for the McKinley boys' Home, which was a charity show, as they have one every year to raise funds for a Christmas dinner and party. The 24th we were scheduled to lead a parade in Long Beach, which is to be the largest parade ever held there - a parade that boasts of 39 bands already entered. We will be working one block ahead of the first unit, putting on our parade drill, with our lights and other electrical gadgets in full blast. The month of December we have two shows all set besides our yearly donation of delivering Christmas baskets to the needy. New Year's morning will find us in Pasadena, where we will again work the Tournament of Roses parade and also the Rose Bowl.

Last week we had the pleasure of entertaining the Portland Police Motorcycle Corps who were enroute to Mexico City for the Police Convention where they will perform along with the drum and bugle corps. We had them over to the clubhouse for our monthly dinner, after showing the sights of Hollywood. They really enjoyed 'slow' ride, didn't you boys? Especially the one to the depot. They were under the command of Capt. Marshall. We certainly enjoyed their visit and hope they had a swell time on their trip. Trooper Hubert Phillips won first prize at our Halloween dance, which makes it two in a row for him. 'Pink Toe Nails' Locke was runner-up. Mrs. Locke won the door prize.

(No author's name given)

**AMA Enthusiast Magazine
March 1940**

"Three up!" In which the west coast representative of the A.M.A., Chet Billings, accepts an invitation to try a stunt. Hap Ruggles drives and Joe Stewart is middle man. A fourth member hooks a ride on the rear stand. Yes, it Is moving – 25 m.p.h.

By Chet Billings

There is no more kicked around term than "Safety." It has been discussed pro and con by police departments, civic groups, various industries, and by the nation. No matter what the approach, the objective is usually the same; get people to thinking safety.

After a three-year safety campaign on the part of the A.M.A., and with increasingly better results having been obtained, we can now do a little analyzing as to safety in motorcycling.

In the January issue we published a set of figures released by the A.M.A. They show, in round numbers, 69,000,000 miles of travel in 1937, the first year of the campaign. In 1938 they show 83,000,000 miles of travel. In 1939 they show 99,000,000 miles of travel. As the miles increased the proportionate number of accidents decreased.

That is all very interesting. In 1937 a certain number of clubs entered a contest to see how far they could travel without an accident. That means first of all that the safety plan had been taken up by groups and not by individuals. Did the same number of clubs travel the additional in miles in 1938. No! The added miles came through more clubs joining the contest. More individuals got in on the group plan.

By the same token more clubs joined the program in 1939. As more people entered the contest, although the number of miles turned greatly increased, the proportion of accidents decreased.

AMA Enthusiast Magazine
March 1940 (Cont'd)

If we could, theoretically, get every motorcycle rider in the U.S. to join a club, which in turn was entered in the safety contest, the accident rate would be lower, in terms of the miles traveled than within any other group that comes within the field of automotive travel.

There are no clubs for car owners. Any safety campaign in that field must make an individual sale to each lone driver. There is no contest or brother members to spur this lone driver on to an active interest. The only contest he is in is one with several million other lone drivers and the awards are life or death.

Actually motorcyclists have made a very enviable record as far as our several hundred clubs are concerned. But does the rest of the U.S. know about it or realize what records we really are setting? The answer once more is very definitely no.

There are several reasons. The public does not get a chance to read the figures for one thing. More important than that, if it did get a chance to read the figures it would still see a picture of our own lone driver, who by now is in the minority but who gets more publicity for his poor showing than the majority gets for a fine showing.

Victor McLaglen is justly proud of the A.M.A. safety award won by the club he has inspired and which won the 39 national championship. Flanked by his ranking officers, he smiles his satisfaction at the police officials who are seen on both sides of the A.M.A representative

One careless motorcycle rider in a town can just about offset the good a whole club can do in that town. People don't notice motors when they are ridden the right way. But when they have to climb trees or lamp posts to dodge the one dare devil they naturally have a very vivid recollection of it.

So it seems that if we are to clinch our safety work we are going to have to do something about the self appointed hell raiser who seems to think he has to show off.

These same clubs that have helped in the first part of the campaign can help in the second part of the campaign. If our dare devil friend is just misguided; if down under the surface he has the makings of what might be called a modern motorcyclist, warm up to him and try to get him interested in club work. If he is a total loss, then there are other ways of dealing with him.

The first thing to do is to see that public officials, civic groups, fraternal organizations and all factions that represent the ear of a city's life are informed of the good side of motorcycling. This is a job in itself. It really constitutes an advertising and a service program.

AMA Enthusiast Magazine
March 1940 (Cont'd)

During the past month the writer was invited to attend a dinner at the Victor McLaglen Sports Center in Los Angeles. The occasion was a formal presentation of the A.M.A. safety award won by the Victor McLaglen Motor Corps for 1939.

A number of influential people had been invited to the dinner including a Captain of the California Highway Patrol and other police officers. During the course of the talks that were given it was pointed out what motorcyclists nationally had done to actively work out this matter of safety. The figures which had been run on page 8 of the January Motorcyclist were read. (We reproduce the same figures again in connection with this article.) They were not just read off in a monotone. They were explained.

All members of the McLaglen Motor Corps have put in many arduous hours of practice during the past four years. Some of their more sensational stunts are the easiest and some of the less spectacular call for real skill. As may be expected one member takes naturally to one kind of a stunt while the next member may take to another. Each is permitted a certain latitude in this respect. On the other hand, each member must practice until he can become a part of their drill team. Here we see Ray Phillips doing a real rope twirling act.

A. M. A. Safety Report

1937
Our members traveled 69,753,000 miles. There were 268 accidents. One accident in 260,027 miles of travel!

1938
Our members traveled 83,567,000 miles. There were 309 accidents.
One accident in 270,443 miles of travel!

1939
Our members traveled 99,469,000 miles.
There were 353 accidents.
One accident in 281,782 miles of travel!

Thus in a short period of three years, our clubs and members have created a safety record that merits due recognition for their efforts to prove that a motorcycle PROPERLY handled is the safest vehicle on the road.

320 Clubs have a perfect record	00
157 Clubs One reportable accident	157
43 Clubs Two reportable accidents	86
21 Clubs Three reportable accidents	63
8 Clubs Four reportable accidents	32
3 Clubs Five reportable accidents	15
56 Clubs Partial reports	....
	Total—353

These clubs reporting represent 15,351 motorcycle riders, giving us an accident percentage of .0229.

Ray Phillips

AMA Enthusiast Magazine
March 1940 (Cont'd)

Then it was brought out that that one club turned some 400,000 miles last year without an accident. It was surprising how surprised some of those visitors were to find out what was going on right under their noses, that they had not noticed or stopped to analyze.

In fact, the Captain of the Patrol admitted that although part of his work was safety, he had not realized what a worth while endeavor this A.M.A. program was or how much of it had been taking place right in his territory. What he did mention was our dare devil friend. He admitted he had probably judged the many by a few.

The Victor McLaglen Motor Corps turned out to be the national champion club in 1939. That didn't just happen. Below we give a list of their public activities since 1936. Attendance figures are necessarily estimated but in many cases these are far too low. For instance, in connection with the Rose Parade in 1939 it shows 100,000. Actually close to two million people gathered to see that Rose Parade. And about 87,000 more gathered to see the famous Rose Bowl football game. Not all of them saw the McLaglen boys who helped the Pasadena police, but certainly more than 100,000.

TOWN	DATE	WHO FOR	Attendance
	1936		
Long Beach	May	Moto-Speedway	3,200
Monterey Park	May (3 days)	Chamber of Commerce	7,500
San Diego	May	World's Fair	8,500
Santa Ana	June	Promoters	6,800
Ventura	Oct.	Promoters	4,000
Brawley	Oct.	Promoters	5,200
Whittier	Oct.	State of Calif.	600
Los Angeles	Nov.	White Sox Park	3,500
Los Angeles	Nov.	Wrigley Field	9,700
Los Angeles	Dec.	(Met Mexican Police in contest. Score Mex. 71, YMMC 91)	7,800
Los Angeles	Dec.	Fox Movietone News	
Hollywood	Dec.	Santa Claus Lane P'de (2 nights)	197,000
	1937		
Pasadena	Jan.	Tournament Roses	850,000
Los Angeles	Jan.	Universal News	
Long Beach	Feb.	C. of C.	160,000
San Bernardino	Mar.	Promoters	5,000
Los Angeles	Mar.	Wrigley Field (2 days)	48,000
Los Angeles	Sept.	National Air Races	180,000
Los Angeles	???	Electrical Parade (Boulder Dam)	270,000
Long Beach	April	Promoters	6,500
Los Angeles	April	Police Show, Coliseum	87,000
Santa Monica	May	Police Dept.	9,000
Las Vegas, Nev.	June	Chamber of Commerce	11,000
Salt Lake City	June	Chamber of Commerce	7,500
Pocatello, Idaho	June	20-30 Club	4,700
Boise, Idaho	June	Police Dept.	5,700
Pendleton, Ore.	June	Round Up Association	126,000
Baker, Ore.	June	Oregon State Patrol	3,800
Portland	June (4 days)	Rose Festival Asso.	840,000
San Francisco	June	Kezar Stadium	15,000
Los Angeles	June	Knights of Columbus	62,000
Los Angeles	July	American Legion	82,000
Los Angeles	July	Jam Handy Productions (for Chevrolet Motor Co.)	
Los Angeles	Aug.	Gilmore Stadium (Midget Races)	18,000
Los Angeles	Aug.	Shriners	12,000
Stockton	Aug.	San Joaquin C'nty Fair	46,000
Sacramento	Sept.	State Fair (2 days)	120,000
Pasadena	Sept.	B.P.O.E. (Rose Bowl)	75,000
Los Angeles	Oct.	Promoters (Gilmore)	2,000
Los Angeles	Nov.	Police (Thanksgiving Benefit)	11,000
Hollywood	Dec.	Santa Claus Lane P'de	60,000
	1938		
Pasadena	Jan.	Rose Parade and Rose Bowl	900,000
Los Angeles	July	Am. Legion (Coliseum)	73,000
Los Angeles	July	Rodeo, Thrill Circus	65,000
Van Nuys	July	State, McKinley Home	350
Los Angeles	Sept.	Wrigley Field, Circus	23,000
Los Angeles	Oct.	State Hi-Way Patrol	4,000
Montebello	Oct.	State Hi-Way Patrol	1,000
Inglewood	Oct.	Chamber of Commerce	1,800
Reno, Nev.	Nov.	Chamber of Commerce	3,500
Los Angeles	Dec.	Police Xmas Benefit	76,000
	1939		
Pasadena	Jan.	Rose Parade and Rose Bowl	900,400
Santa Anita	July	Sheriff's Barbecue	35,000
Van Nuys	Aug.	Hugh Herbert Rodeo	4,000
Los Angeles	July (3 days)	Police Show (Coliseum)	86,000
Los Angeles	June	Hal Roach Show	400
Los Angeles	Oct.	Thanksgiving Show	5,700
Glendale	Feb.	Scots Day	???????
Los Angeles	Mar.	Promoters (White Sox)	3,500
Los Angeles	June	Promoters (Coliseum) Rodeo	18,000
Pasadena	July	Elks Show (Rose Bowl)	?????
Long Beach	Aug.	City (Parade)	85,000
Los Angeles	Dec.	Xmas Benefit (City)	5,000
	1940		
Pasadena	Jan.	Rose Parade and Rose Bowl	100,000
Los Angeles	Feb.	Arturo Godoy	100
Los Angeles	Mar.	Promoter	
San Bernardino	Mar.	Promoter	

**AMA Enthusiast Magazine
March 1940 (Cont'd)**

The list shows how hard that club worked, and how long it worked before it made the grade and was selected national champion club. And it also shows that despite all the people who saw them perform, there are also many who do not know they exist or what fine work they are doing.

So it is essential that clubs be constantly alert to inform their own localities of the records they are accomplishing. Take figures like these from the A.M.A. and see that they get into the hands of as many people as possible in your community. Then live up to the figures.

Try to get as many riders into clubs as possible. They don't have to all belong to one club. Too many members make a club top heavy. Cooperate and start other clubs. Cooperate with the new clubs. Push them out in front and see that they are helped to learn all the things the experienced club knows. Then when the wheat has been cleaned from the chaff, thoroughly ostracize the guy who still has to be the show off. He may barge through town and demoralize traffic on the highway without getting pinched. The officers may not even know where to find him. But you do. You know his machine, his name and all his habits. So do something about it.

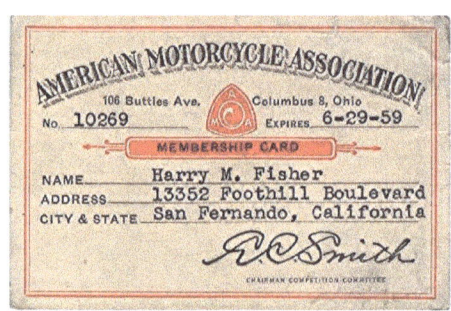

Sample A.M.A. membership card

**A.M.A. decal for
Life Members**

The Enthusiast Magazine
April 1940
Page 12

Hail to the NATIONAL A.M.A. CLUB CONTEST WINNERS!

During the past month the writer was invited to attend a dinner at the Victor McLaglen Sports Center in Los Angeles. The occasion was a formal presentation of the A.M.A. safety award won by the Victor McLaglen Motor Corps for 1939.

We are proud to show these pictures of the winners of the 1939 A.M.A. National Club Contest..... #1. First place went to the Victor McLaglen Motorcycle Corps, Los Angeles.

The Enthusiast Magazine
August 1940
Pgs. 18-19

McLAGLEN MCY. CORPS, Los Angeles, Calif. --- "We have been having real motorcycling weather out here lately. In fact, it has been quite warm. We had a lovely time down in Chinatown last week (we have a new one here now). We had a dinner, dance, concessions, etc. Last Saturday we had a 49'er night at the club and drew 450 paid admissions at 40c a head. What a night! Friday night we attended the wedding of one of our charter members, and right after that, we were escorted to Pasadena to the Rose Bowl, where we put on a show with the Tournament of Roses Band (the band we went on tour with in 1937). We closed the show that night and then on the Fourth we went to the Coliseum with the American Legion for their annual big show. The end of July we are scheduled to appear at the Santa Anita Race Track for the sheriff's department, helping with their annual barbecue dinner, which draws around 65,000 persons each year. The Police Show is next month, but the exact date is unknown at present. This will make the fourth year we have been in that show.

 Editor note: The 6th annual Police Show was held on August 16, 1940 with Attendence of 75,000.

The Enthusiast Magazine
September 1940
Page 18

VICTOR McLAGLEN MCY. CORPS, Los Angeles, Calif. --- "Greetings to all clubs. Here's a little information all you riders may find of interest. If you have been planning to start a drill team or have one already and want some new maneuvers, be sure to see one of Warner Brothers' latest pictures entitled 'Meet John Doe.' This picture stars Gary Cooper, Barbara Stanwyck, Edward Arnold, and Rod LaRoque. We are proud to say that our troop puts on its drills from beginning to end with close-ups of the more ticklish maneuvers. No date has been set for the release of this picture as yet, but watch for it because we think it will really interest you a lot"

The Enthusiast Magazine
December 1940
Page 22

Victor McLaglen News

LOS ANGELES, Calif. – As the year is winding up and a new one will soon be here, the Victor McLaglen Motorcycle Corps has been "hit" with parades between now and New Year's more than ever. On November the 20th we headed the Xmas holiday parade in downtown Los Angeles which was seven miles long. On the 22nd we headed a parade in Long Beach, California, during their "Festival of Bands" where they had sixty-seven various musical organizations, all trying for first prize. This parade attracted a crowd, the largest that ever turned out in that particular city. New Year's Eve will find us in Santa Ana riding at the head of their annual Santa Ana Frolic. Last year was the first year and we headed the parade and won the grand sweepstakes prize. This parade was witnessed by 65,000 persons.

On all these parades where we headed them we ride back and forth in a block length, putting on our lighted street drill.

The biggest day of the year, where we have our hands full, and have done the job for the past five years, is in Pasadena on New Year's Day. We "spot" the floats in their respective positions for the parade and after the parade moves it is our job not to let it stop. This all happens the morning after the Santa Ana affair, so it looks like no celebrating the New Year for all the boys????

On the night of November 7th we put on our show in the Rose Bowl for the Tournament of Roses which draws about 13,000 persons. This is for the Pasadena Jr. College fund.

The night of last November 16th International Truckmen's Association held their "rodeo" in Los Angeles and the annual contest was held for the champion truck driver of the United States, the winner being a lad from Indianapolis, Indiana. Stand up, you "Hoosiers," and take a bow, you really have a champion. The way he throws that "cat and semi" around is nobody's business. We put on a fifteen-minute show for the visiting truckmen and their families, which drew around 9000 persons. After that we had a big dinner tendered us, and which the chief of police of L.A. also attended.

We have started to map out our plans now for our '41 drill. It has been a proven fact that changing the drill routine every year keeps the people guessing what we will do next. We will no doubt keep the four-way cross-over, as that one brings them to their feet. Captain DeRush has been very busy lately running back and forth to the studio pertaining to the release of "Meet John Doe" which will be next month. Until next year we say "Adios 1940," "Hello '41."

- Hap

The Enthusiast Magazine
May 1941
Page 15

VICTOR McLAGLEN MOTORCYCLE CORPS,
Los Angeles, Calif. --- "We attended an advance showing of the new film 'Meet John Doe' in which we put on some of our best stunts. Originally 2700 feet of film were taken of our drills, and naturally we were very much dismayed to find out that only 60 feet of our original 2700 feet will be shown in the finished movie. We felt bad until we heard that the cutting room left out 18000 feet of film originally shot and so now we don't feel quite so bad.

We had the honor of appearing at the premiere of the picture through an invitation from Warner Bros. along with the stars and the who's who of Hollywood on the night of the 12th of March. Incidentally, most of the country knows that a premiere out here in Hollywood is quite an event. It certainly was a night of thrills for us. We're looking forward to appearing at the Northern California Rally to be held the end of May."

Hap Ruggles

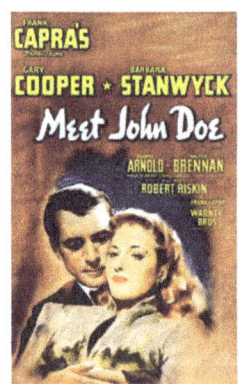

"Suicide Split" as filmed for this movie

"4-Way Crossover"

The Enthusiast Magazine
July 1941
Page 17

*VICTOR McLAGLEN MCY. CORPS, Los Angeles, Calif. ---
"Well, Hollister and the District 36 Gypsy Tour and Rally have come and gone, and through this column our gang wants to thank all of the Northern California riders, the clubs, dealers, officials and the Hollister folks, for it was indeed a pleasure for us to travel the great distance up there and put on our show and to be received with such an ovation This rally was the best-handled affair that we believe we have ever attended. To all the committees, Especially George Harris, Chet Billings, Pop Cohen, Dud Perkins, and the Bay City Club, we salute you. May next year's rally be as good as this one – it can't be better, the way everybody worked. A word to Capt. Fred Marshall and his boys who drove from Portland, Oregon, to watch us work. We certainly enjoyed their companionship. The Portland Police Drill Team are an expert aggregation and we were glad we had a chance to be with them. A large bouquet of orchids to the Renard Sisters, who put on a real bunch of stunts at the rally. Hollister will always remain one of our most pleasant memories."*

At 8:00 o'clock one of the big features of the rally was scheduled. Long before that hour, every seat in the stands and every point of vantage around the fence was jammed. Promptly on the hour, the famous stunt team of the Victor McLaglen Motorcycle Corps rolled out onto the field led by Truman DeRush. A mighty roar went up from the assemblage, testifying to the fame of this great aggregation,

For one solid hour the crowed sat spellbound as the incomparable McLaglen Motorcycle stunt team performed in sensational fashion. During the first half-hour, the floodlights of the Park were turned off and colorful red, green, and blue lights flickered from each machine as the McLaglenites went through their difficult maneuvers. They did pinwheels, wheeling their mounts around in small circles, pushups, they rode backwards, in pyramids with three to nine men on one machine, they did handstands and many more seemingly impossible stunts. In a nine-man pyramid they arched over two motorcycles and with six motorcycles traveling side by side, the 21 men moved across the field. Their show came to a thrilling close as the entire troop of 21 men who weigh 3,468 pounds, rode slowly past the stands on a Harley-Davidson, a new record for multiple transportation on a solo job.

Hap Ruggles

The Enthusiast Magazine
January 1942
Page 16

VICTOR McLAGLEN MCY. CORPS, Los Angeles, Calif. --- This year has nearly gone and it has been one of the busiest in the history of the Motor Corps. We traveled close to 600,000 motorcycle miles, and as Santa Claus will be pulling into town now pretty soon, we are busy preparing for the Tournament of Roses Parade. November was a busy month for us with parades besides having two shows for the month we also led the Christmas Parade downtown in Los Angeles and also the mammoth Festival of Bands in Long Beach where 67 various musical organizations paraded. This particular parade is held annually and was witnessed by 350,000 persons.

At our last open house we went roller skating and most of the members were down more than they were up. Our next open house we are going to Earl Carroll's for a party. We are now preparing a big Christmas get-together with the proceeds to be used for Christmas baskets for the needy. We hope to give about 18 baskets this year if our plans pan out. It is our great moment presenting those baskets to the needy and take it from us it is not a happy job especially where there are children in the home. We have four new members, Fenton, Burry, Raizer and Riley and we welcome them into our fold. This brings the membership up to 29 men even if Uncle Sam did take 8 of our members. Three of them are now motorcycle instructors. Plans are going ahead to remodel our club house and grounds in the near future with the building of a foreign city within our grounds and the plans call for the changing of the foreign city or village about four times a year. This will not affect our drill field. It is a great and unique idea and should be very interesting to all those who come to our grounds.

Hap Ruggles

Staff Sergeant Edwin Kuhn of the Camp Roberts, Calif., Quartermaster Motor Pool "gasses up" a Harley-Davidson as pretty Phyllis Schroeder, civilian employe of the Motor Pool office, poses in the saddle. She has been chosen as a "Roberts Rose," selected by the Camp Roberts DISPATCH, as one of the most beautiful young women at the Post. Public Relations Photo, Camp Roberts.

but these two seem to be his favorite. He has written several songs which are hits, one of the latest being *"Ft. Worth Jail"*. Dick said he owned a Harley-Davidson before going to Hollywood. He said it felt good to be back in the saddle again, when I took his picture astride my 61. Another nice personality of the show was "Shorty" Long who is the target for all the fellows' jokes. He is older than the rest of the boys on the show and supplies everyone with plenty of laughs. "Shorty" is a very likeable fellow and told me that he works for Metro Goldwyn Mayer Studios in Hollywood. He posed for a picture reading a script just as he does on the air. He always wears a red shirt so that he can be easily distinguished from the rest of the boys.

A favorite among the members of the cast is the pretty girl singer who is not only pleasing to look at but also has a very excellent singing voice. Her name is Miss Virginia Vass. Virginia posed for a couple of nice pictures, one of which was on my 61 and it was the first time, she said, she had ever been on a motorcycle, but she enjoyed it. She is a member of the famous Vass family of stage, screen and radio fame, and had already gained national recognition before joining Gene Autry's Melody Ranch group. I was sorry that my camera was not able to record color at the moment because the Melody Ranch Boys and Virginia wore royal blue costumes and looked very nice.

Later we rode about eleven miles east to Gene Autry, Okla., a small town of a few hundred inhabitants. I well remember this place on November 18, back in 1941 when around 100,000 people visited the town when its name was changed from Berwyn to Gene Autry in honor of the cowboy star because he had bought an 11,000 acre ranch a few miles west

---

OUR COVER PHOTO

OH BOY! Here are two of Hollywood's most glamorous — Rita Hayworth and Betty Grable. The enchanted young men with the "up-in-the-clouds" expressions are members of the Victor McLaglen Motor Corps. The occasion was the recent charity football game between the comedians and leading men of Hollywood. The Motor Corps, thirty strong, performed some of their most intricate formations and drills for the assembled thousands. Oh Boy! — California here we come!

**The Enthusiast Magazine
February 1948
Pages 12-13**

VICTOR McLAGLEN MCY. CORPS, Los Angeles, Calif. --- Happy New Year, to all of you! Our roll call is now answered by 28 members with three on the 30-day probation period. Recent performances were given at Downey, California, for the High School between halves of the All Southwestern Championship game, and on November 26, we journeyed to Hollywood, where we led the Santa Claus Parade.

On November 27, Thanksgiving, we performed at the Coliseum in the preview for the football game between the Dons and the Cleveland Browns. On December 6, we were at Long Beach leading the All Western Band Review parade. Nothing but music, brass bands, drum corps, etc. On New Year's eve we journeyed to Santa Ana to lead their annual frolic parade, which saw 150,000 Orange County citizens viewing their mammoth parade. After the parade we were the guests of Jack Wager and Joe Walker the Harley-Davidson dealers, and they are two guys who KNOW HOW TO PUT ON A PARTY. Thanks men, we will never forget that party even if we didn't get any sleep before Pasadena, where we had roll call at 5:00 A.M.

This was the big day of the Pasadena Rose Parade which makes the tenth parade we have worked in. For you eastern lads and lasses, the parade is divided into divisions, and two or three of us are assigned to each division, and once the parade "kicks off" it is our job to keep it moving, and if any float breaks down it is up to us to get it off to the side or get a tow car to pull it. We each have maps where we can put our finger on a tow car, ambulance, gas truck, service truck, first aid station, or any other needed equipment. Well anyway – it was a great day and a great parade. And for you fellows in Michigan, you sure have a great team.

We have our complete new uniforms now and we have our wheels with the lights all hooked up, along with our chrome helmets. We made our first electrical appearance for the Santa Claus parade. Also we have a television show in March and two in April. The next item I send in will give the members' names as some of our boys are from back east, and perhaps you would like to get in touch with them. In response to our previous article in the ENTHUSIAST, we received any letter and we hope to receive more from time to time.

Capt. Hap Ruggles, secy.
610 ½ Venice Blvd.

**The Enthusiast Magazine
January 1949
Page 15**

Nowhere in the world does Santa Claus arrive with such pomp and ceremony as he does in Hollywood. Among the famous folk who helped escort Santa through the streets of the movie capital were Bob Hope, Doris Day and four members of the McLaglen Motorcycle Corps, W. Bengstrom (left), . Rayzor, S. Eastin and Sid Allen.

Photo – Hyman Fink at PHOTOPLAY.

The Enthusiast Magazine
February 1949
Cover and Pages 2-5 & 22-23

McLaglen Motorcycle Corps ROLLS AGAIN

THE Corps is back in the saddle again —rolling along to fresh achievements and adding an exciting new chapter to an already colorful history. Inactive during the war years, the Corps is operating once more with greater flash, greater splendor and new equipment.

The Corps still carries the original name it started out with, but today, only two of the charter members are still in the organization — Major Nick DeRush and Captain Hap Ruggles. And the present sponsor is the Harley-Davidson dealer of Los Angeles, Rich Budelier.

In 1935 the Corps was formed by DeRush and Ruggles. Frank McCartney, another well-known West Coast motorcycle figure, gave them a hand in getting started. Soon Victor McLaglen, the rugged movie star, incorporated the group as a unit into his McLaglen Lighthorse Troop, and the Corps was on its way. Its reputation grew swiftly. It traveled up and down the Coast thrilling spectators by the thousands. The members practiced hard and long, and gradually added new stunts and maneuvers to their bag of tricks.

When the Corps first began, it served merely as an escort at smaller functions while it gained experience, but it wasn't too long before the boys were able to put on an entire show. The demand for their services grew, and soon they were appearing in San Francisco, at the San Diego Fair, at Hollywood, the Rose Bowl and even beyond the borders of their native state. Each succeeding year saw the Corps improve and expand its show. The constant practice brought the members always a little closer to that perfection of rhythm and timing which they already possessed to an unusual degree. It might be noted in passing, that all during the life of the McLaglen Motorcycle Corps, the personnel has relied on Harley-Davidsons to help them perform their maneuvers.

Among highlights of those early years were their appearances at the world-famous Rose Bowl Parade; at the great Electrical Pageant celebrating the opening of Boulder Dam; at the Los Angeles Policemen's Benefit Show before 60,000 fans, and their historic performance when they were pitted against the famed Mexico City Police Stunt Team, which had built an enviable record by its stunts, also performed on Harley-Davidson motorcycles. The Mexicans arrived in California in 1936 on an extended goodwill

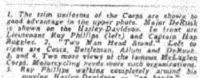

1. *This fancy stunt is called "The Belt Hold On." Bill Lewis holds the belts of Fenton and Allum. Charles Griggs is in front, Greenwood in back and Hap Ruggles is pilot. 2. McLaglen Corps, on black and white Harley-Davidsons, leads the "All Western Band Review" parade at Long Beach. 3. Bengston pushes up Ray Phillips.*

1. *The trim uniforms of the Corps are shown to good advantage in the upper photo. Major DeRush is shown on the Harley-Davidson. In front are Lieutenant Ray Phillips (left) and Captain Hap Ruggles. 2. "Two Man Head Stand." Left to right are Costa, Bettleman, Allum and DeRush. 3, and 4. Two more views of the famous McLaglen Corps. Motorcycling needs more such organizations. 5. Ray Phillips walking completely around his moving Harley-Davidson — "no hands."*

tour. Their great reputation as champion stunt artists had preceded them, and when they had arrived, the McLaglen Corps promptly issued a friendly challenge. The visitors smiled and accepted with pleasure.

It was an exciting day when the two organizations met. The stands were packed! For hours the Mexicans and the McLaglenites thrilled the crowd with their difficult stunts and complicated maneuvers. Points were awarded for balance, speed, falls and ability in performing stunts. When the afternoon was over, the McLaglen Corps emerged as victors by a score of 91 to 72. It was indeed a day DeRush and Ruggles will never forget, and that performance is now part of the tradition of the Corps.

With the reorganization of the Corps following World War II, the members blossomed out with late model black and white Harley-Davidsons and new blue and gold uniforms. Eisenhower jackets, gold-trimmed pockets, shoulder patches, wings on each lapel, and cadet style caps with gold or silver band on the bill of the cap, depending on the rank of the wearer. A white scarf is also worn with the uniform. Breeches are dark blue with gold stripes. On drills and parades, the boys wear chromed helmets. The Harley-Davidsons are equipped with wheel lights, since half of the drills are done in darkness.

The Corps holds at least six practice sessions each month, in addition to its parades and shows. At the present time, the following members belong to the organization: Nick DeRush, Hap Ruggles, Ray Phillips, Otto Locke, John Greenwood, Sidney Allen, James Fenton, Frank Blaesser, Harold Bettleman, Virgil Ervin, Sterling Eastin, Edward Bengston, Harvey Behling, James Parsons, Fernando Palomarez, William Allum, Ken Rayzor, Stanley Kemp, Don Bignell, LeVern Tegg— *(Please turn to Page 22)*

1. and 2. Photographer Hyman Fink of Photoplay Magazine got these two shots on the night the McLaglen Corps led the Santa Claus Parade. In the first photo are Arthur Lake and Penny Singleton of the movies with Ralph Edwards, of radio fame, gives the boys a laugh. 3. "Three Of A Kind"— Ray Phillips (front) Bengston and Greenwood. 4. Ray Phillips does a difficult jump from rear stand to seat. 5. "The Horse" — Ed Phillips up, and Harold Bettleman at the handlebars.

1. *This stunt is called a "Ladder Head Stand." John Greenwood is in front, Sterling Eastin is at the controls, Lawrence Kenton is in the rear and Leo Costa is upside down. 2. "Three High." Costa at the bars, Benson and Ed Phillips on top. In the rear is Eastin. 3. and 4. The wonderful balancing qualities of the Corps' Harley-Davidsons are demonstrated by Greenwood (top) and Ray Phillips. 5. Cal. Kuit of The McLaglen Lighthorse Troop receives trophy from American Legion. Ruggles and DeRush in background. Braun Photo.*

**The Enthusiast Magazine
February 1949
Pages 2-5 & 22-23**

The Corps is back in the saddle again – rolling along to fresh achievements and adding an exciting new chapter to an already colorful history. In-active during the war years, the Corps is operating once more with greater flash, greater splendor and new equipment.

The Corps still carries the original name it started out with, but today, only two of the charter members are still in the organization – Major Nick DeRush and Captain Hap Ruggles. And the present sponsor is the Harley-Davidson dealer of Los Angeles, Rich Budelier.

In 1935 the Corps was formed by DeRush and Ruggles. Frank McCartney, another well-known West Coast motorcycle figure, gave them a hand in getting started. Soon Victor McLaglen, the rugged movie star, incorporated the group as a unit into his McLaglen Lighthorse Troop, and the Corps was on its way. Its reputation grew swiftly. It traveled up and down the Coast thrilling spectators by the thousands. The members practiced hard and long, and gradually added new stunts and maneuvers to their bag of tricks.

When the Corps first began, it served merely as an escort at smaller functions while it gained experience, but it wasn't too long before the boys were able to put on an entire show. The demand for their services grew, and soon they were appearing in San Francisco, at the San Diego Fair, at Hollywood, the Rose Bowl and even beyond the borders of their native state. Each succeeding year saw the Corps improve and expand its show. The constant practice brought the members always a little closer to that perfection of rhythm and timing which they already possessed to an unusual degree. It might be noted in passing, that all during the life of the McLaglen Motorcycle Corps, the personnel has relied on Harley-Davidsons to help them perform their maneuvers.

Among highlights of those early years were their appearances at the world-famous Rose Bowl Parade; at the great Electrical Pageant celebrating the opening of Boulder Dam; at the Los Angeles Policemen' Benefit Show before 60,000 fans, and their historic performance when they were pitted against the famed Mexico City Police Stunt Team, which had built an enviable record by its stunts, also performed on Harley-Davidson motorcycles. The Mexicans arrived in California in 1936 on an extended goodwill tour. Their great reputation as champion stunt artists had preceded them, and when they had arrived, the McLaglen Corps promptly issued a friendly challenge. The visitors smiled and accepted with pleasure.

It was an exciting day when the two organizations met. The stands were packed for hours! The Mexicans and the McLaglenites thrilled the crowd with their difficult stunts and complicated maneuvers. Points were awarded for balance, speed, falls and ability in performing stunts. When the afternoon was over, the McLaglen Corps emerged as victors by a score of 91 to 72. It was indeed a day DeRush and Ruggles will never forget and that performance is now part of the tradition of the Corps.

With the reorganization of the Corps following World War II, the members blossomed out with late model black and white Harley-Davidsons and new blue and gold uniforms, Eisenhower jackets, gold-trimmed pockets, shoulder patches, wings on each lapel, and cadet style caps with gold or silver on the band on the bill of the cap, depending on the rank of the wearer. A white scarf is also worn with the uniform. Breeches are dark blue with gold stripes. On drills and parades, the boys wear chromed helmets. The Harley-Davidsons are equipped with wheel lights, since half of the drills are done in darkness.

The Corps holds at least six practice sessions each month, in addition to its parades and shows. At the present time, the following members belong to the organization: Nick DeRush, Hap Ruggles, Ray Phillips, Otto Locke, John Greenwood, Sidney Allen, James Fenton, Frank Blaesser, Harold Bettleman, Virgil Ervin, Sterling Eastin, Edward Bengston, Harvey Behling, James Parsons, Fernando Palomares, Willliam Allum, Ken Rayzor, Stanley Kemp, Don Bignell, LeVern Tegland, Rolls Butler, Don Block, Phil Erickson, Bob Hasselbring, Edwin Phillips, William Lewis, Pete Cromer, Lawrence Benton, Lorin Haynes, Elmo Dyerly, Charles Griggs, Vern Widdup and Leo Costa. They come from all walks of life, but they have one thing in common – enthusiasm, plus a special skill when it comes to handling a motorcycle.

Among recent high spots in the McLaglen Corps' history are the following parades: Santa Claus in Hollywood, March of Dimes, Western Band Review, American Legion, Santa Ana Fun Frolic, Professional Football Opening, numerous charity appearances, and, of course, the most famous of all – the Tournament of Roses Parade. Last fall, when the presidential candidates of both political parties appeared in Los Angeles, the Corps was given a few minutes to put on several of their choice stunts.
(Editor note: Presidential candidates: Harry S. Truman, Democrat and Thomas E. Dewey, Republican.)

The spectacular Santa Claus Parade and the colorful Rose Parade give the McLaglen Corps the most strenuous workouts. The night that Santa Claus makes his first triumphant ride down Hollywood Boulevard, the Corps has five minutes to do some of its special drills before the parade "kicks off." Hollywood Boulevard is "all theirs" and the hundreds of thousands lining the Boulevard get a real thrill watching the Corps in action. "And we're thrilled too," says Captain Ruggles. "Who wouldn't be, in front of those hundreds of thousands?"

The parade this year was super – filled with beautiful floats – 20 bands – 300 horses with silver saddles and equipment, and, of course, headed by Santa Claus and his reindeer. Movie stars twinkle brilliantly throughout the line of the parade with blonde Doris Day riding alongside Mr. Claus – the lucky guy!

The Corps members go into action at 5:00 A.M., at Pasadena, on the memorable day of the Tournament of Roses. This year marked their eighth appearance in this great Rose Parade. Incidentally, theirs is the only motorcycle group to work in this parade.

"No stunts on a day like this for the Corps," says Captain Ruggles. "Our job is to escort and to patrol. We are charged with the responsibility of seeing that the floats are in their proper places, and the bands, horse troops and all the other parade aides are in their designated spots. A mountain of pre-parade details to be ironed out is really something to cause despair and confusion, but we are able to handle our job smoothly, thanks to the splendid cooperation we get from all the parade officials and participants. Once the colorful spectacle gets under way, our Corps members patrol up and down the line of march, carefully watching all floats. In case of a breakdown, the crippled float is quickly removed to a side street and the colorful parade moves on without an interruption.

"We're always ready for trouble," remarks Captain Hap Ruggles, "and as a result, it's never nearly as bad as we anticipate. Plenty of preparation beforehand is our strongest weapon.

After more than a dozen years of stunting, drilling and escorting, it might be expected that the McLaglenites have received many tributes, and they have. The trophy case in their clubroom at 4408 West Jefferson Boulevard is crowded with cups and banners won during the years. In 1939, the McLaglen Corps won the American Motorcycle Association National Club Activity Contest – the highest honor in American motorcycling circles. Fame has come to the Corps in other ways too. They have appeared before the newsreel camera on a number of occasions and expect to appear in a short movie feature tentatively titled, "Wheels and Wheels," Many movie stars have been snapped surrounded by Corps members, and autographed pictures from celebrities, in many fields, line the Corps clubroom walls. The members meet on Wednesday nights, after rehearsal in their clubroom at 4408 West Jefferson Boulevard, where the welcome mat is always out to visiting motorcyclists.

Plans for the future may include trips as far inland as the Middle West. The offers are many, but the members have personal obligations and problems to consider. After all, they leave their regular jobs during the week – the Corps is their hobby on weekends. Surely, they deserve to go on a national tour. The entire country ought to see the McLaglen Corps in action. A national tour might inspire other clubs to attempt similar drill and stunt organizations. Crack stunt and drill teams could well be started throughout the country to focus attention on the finer aspects of the sport of motorcycling. The McLaglen Corps has done a magnificent job on the West Coast in gaining the respect and the admiration of the public. Here, indeed, is a challenge to other clubs to follow the McLaglen Corps' example in fostering good public relations. How many clubs will take advantage of this golden opportunity?

(No author shown)

EPILOGUE - The Beginning of the END. . . Eight Years Later

You're probably wondering, *"What's the Motor Corps doing now?"* Here we are eight years after Harry's death and six years since the previous two books were published. This is my take on where we are in 2022.

In 2014, after Commander Harry left us, the team met and voted to have Scott Griffin serve as Drill Leader. Mark Frymoyer continued his position as Stunt Leader and Father Frank got busier with all the paperwork. I dropped out and just offered advice when asked. The team performed in a bunch of shows and continued practices.

Four years later, Scott resigned his position and Mark was voted in as the new Drill Leader. Mark continues to do a terrific job of keeping the momentum going and the great reputation of the Victor McLaglen Motor Corps intact. A great example was when Mark successfully negotiated with the Harley-Davidson Motor Company event planner, Erica Kaponya, to perform for their "Wild Ones: Vintage Motorcycle Rally" in Milwaukee, Wisconsin. The event took place on Saturday, July 13, 2019, and there were three shows on that hot, humid day. Mark was able to talk all the active members and a couple of the not-so-active members into taking this trip, and they had 13 members performing (plus me). Even though I considered myself retired from the team, I agreed to attend and announce for the team. What the heck? Patrick and I were planning a road trip to Maine, so why not just swing by Milwaukee on the way!

The shows were a huge success and Erica, Harley's Event Coordinator, provided our members, a personalized tour of the Harley Museum and back rooms. We were very impressed and loved looking at all those old Harleys. The Motor Corps even had a display in the main part of the museum.

"Ladder-Scissors-Speedo"
Front Fender: Erica

We are proud to have been a part of this rally and appreciative to Erica for arranging all the particulars of our stay. It was great fun!

It was trips like this one that made being a member of this great team such a pleasure. Showing off in front of other motorcycle enthusiasts, riding those terrific machines, traveling to new places and enjoying the camaraderie of the other members – what more enjoyment could there be?

EPILOGUE (Cont'd)

    Unfortunately, COVID-19 struck in the beginning of 2020 and that was devastating for many, including the Motor Corps. Promoters canceled all events and we didn't even get together to practice for fear we would spread the disease among our members. That was pretty much the story for 2020 and 2021.

    Now, we're in 2022 and most of our members have gone on to other pursuits or have jobs that are more demanding. The Motor Corps is a big commitment, and takes a lot of time, energy and finances. It's impossible for everyone to give up their weekends for practices and shows, or pay for uniform and motorcycle maintenances, or travel, etc. After being dormant for two years, it is clear the momentum has dwindled. It takes a lot to get the enthusiasm and passion going again.

    Sadly, the Victor McLaglen Motor Corps "*ain't what she use to be!*" Unfortunately, it may take some time to get the show "*on the road again.*" On the other hand, maybe one of the members' kids might just catch the **Motor Corps show bug** and bring it up to speed again! One never knows.

Ruth Fisher
VMMC, Retired

www.ingramcontent.com/pod-product-compliance
Lightning Source LLC
Chambersburg PA
CBHW080848020526
44118CB00037B/2303